A Stranger in My House

A Stranger In My House

JEWS AND ARABS IN THE WEST BANK

Walter Reich

Firethorn Press

First published in Great Britain in 1985 by
Waterstone & Co Limited
49 Hay's Mews, London W1X 7RT.

Firethorn Press is an imprint of
Waterstone & Co Limited

ISBN: 0–947752–22–6

Distributed by Sidgwick & Jackson Limited
1 Tavistock Chambers
Bloomsbury Way
London WC1A 2SG

Printed in Great Britain by A. Wheaton & Co. Ltd, Exeter

For my parents,
Simon and Anna Reich,
who have known passion and loss

And they told him and said: We came to the land where you sent us, and indeed it flows with milk and honey, and this is its fruit. . . . And they gave the children of Israel an evil report on the land which they had spied out, saying: The land through which we passed as spies is a land that consumes its inhabitants. . . .

Numbers 13:27–32

Contents

The West Bank Then and Now

Ira Rapaport, once of Brooklyn, pulled his small Peugeot to the shoulder of a narrow, steep road twenty miles north of Jerusalem. "We're in the heart of Samaria," he said, adjusting the knitted yarmulke on his head. "The world calls this the West Bank. The Arabs call it part of Palestine. The stone terraces covering every hill for miles around were built by my grandfathers in the days of our kings and our prophets. This is where David ran from Saul. On that hill Judah Maccabee sprang a trap on an occupying Syrian army many times the size of his and won Jewish independence. North of here, in Shechem, which the Arabs call Nablus, Abraham made his first stop in Canaan, and Joshua his farewell address. On the other side of those hills is Shiloh, where we've just built a Jewish settlement, where I live with my wife and children, and where, three thousand years ago, we made our first capital and became a people. This is a place from which we were repeatedly expelled and to which we repeatedly returned. And now we've returned once again. We're back to stay. This is Israel. This is my home."

Rapaport, forty years old, is one of some 45,000 Jews who have settled in the West Bank so far — in the part north of Jerusalem, which they call by its biblical name, Samaria, and in the part south of the city, which they call Judea. They have estalished more than 120 settlements, the great majority of

1

them in the past five years. Some Israeli experts predict a population of 100,000 Jewish settlers in the West Bank by 1990.

Some of the Jewish settlements are communal and self-sustaining in nature. Made up of fifty to a hundred families each, they are populated by Jews, perhaps a quarter of them immigrants from the United States and other Western countries, who, like Rapaport, feel powerful religious and historical ties to the land. Other settlements are, for the time being, more like small towns. Though planned as cities that will have populations of 50,000 or more and that will also have their own industries, they now serve as bedroom communities for Israelis working in Tel Aviv and Jerusalem. In fact, because of the West Bank's small size (about that of greater Los Angeles) and location (at the very center of Israel, nearly all of it within a few miles of the country's main population centers), the territory is a natural and logical place for Israeli urban growth.

Or it would be were it not for the complicating factor of politics. The vast majority of the West Bank's population — about 750,000 people — is not Israeli but Arab. And as far as that majority is concerned, Israelis have no business being there.

What brought them there was the Six-Day War, in 1967. On the first day of that war, Israel notified King Hussein of Jordan that if he held back his forces, and refrained from joining Egypt and Syria in the fighting, Israel would hold its own fire against him. He did not, Israel responded, and within three days the Jewish state found itself in possession of the eastern part of Jerusalem, as well as the West Bank, both of which Jordan had seized and occupied in the 1948–1949 Arab-Israeli war.

Earlier in the century what is now known as the West Bank was a very small part of the territory, located on both sides of the Jordan River, known as Palestine. That territory had been taken from Turkey by the victorious First World War Allies and had been assigned to British administration by the League of Nations as the British Mandate for Palestine. In 1921 Britain's colonial secretary, Winston Churchill, authorized that the part of Palestine lying to the east of the Jordan River, amounting to more than three quarters of the territory, be administered by Abdullah, the non-Palestinian son of the sharif of Mecca, who had marched into the area with a private army. This part of Palestine, known as eastern Palestine, or Transjordan, became in 1921 the Emirate of Transjordan, and then, in 1946, the independent Hashemite Kingdom of Transjordan, with Abdullah, the grandfather of the current king, Hussein, first its emir and then its king; in 1949, the country was renamed the Hashemite Kingdom of Jordan. The remaining one quarter of Palestine, to the west of the river, was by 1922 the part to which the term "Palestine," or "the British Mandate for Palestine," was restricted.

Some years before, in 1917, Great Britain had issued its famous Balfour Declaration, in which it had promised that the Jewish people would have a homeland in Palestine. According to one plan, that homeland was to be made up of western Palestine as well as a part of eastern Palestine, up to the Hejaz railway, which ran in a north-south line from Turkey through Damascus and Amman down to Mecca. Churchill's decision to give all of eastern Palestine to Abdullah—which he made, as he would wryly remember, "one Sunday afternoon in Jerusalem"—rendered that plan impossible. All that was left of Palestine as a potential Jewish homeland was the western part, a fraction of the original whole. The Arabs were relieved by Churchill's fateful decision, and Abdullah himself observed, with satisfaction, that "He [God] granted me success in creating the Government of Transjordan by having it separated from the Balfour Declaration."

In 1947, when the time finally came to establish the Jewish homeland, the United Nations decided to do so by dividing the remaining part of Palestine in two. One section was assigned to the Jews, one to the Arabs. Though some Jewish leaders, such as Menachem Begin, felt bitter about this "second partition" of Palestine, which left them with only a small segment, about 17 percent, of the original territory, the vast majority of Jews accepted it.

The Arabs, however, both the local ones and the ones in the surrounding states, did not. As soon as the State of Israel was announced in 1948, five Arab armies attacked it. The Israeli forces fought back and, as a result of the fighting, managed not only to hold on to the territory the Jews had been assigned but also to capture some they had not. The parts of western Palestine controlled by Arab armies at the time of the 1949 armistice included the areas that came to be called the West Bank and the Gaza Strip. Jordan occupied the former and Egypt the latter.

In 1948 all Jews in Jordanian-occupied East Jerusalem, including all Jews in the Old City's Jewish quarter, fled, as did all Jews in the West Bank; thereafter none lived in those regions or, indeed, in Jordan itself. At the same time, several hundred thousand Arabs fled Israel into Jordan, the West Bank, Gaza, Syria, Lebanon, and other areas. Some of these Arabs were granted citizenship by their host countries, especially Jordan, and they settled in permanent homes. Others, however, were not granted permanent citizenship and were instead kept as refugees; their assimilation, it was feared, would lead in the long run to the acceptance of the new, unwanted state, on what was considered to be immutably Arab soil. Ironically, some of those who fled the area that became Israel in 1948 were Arabs, or the descendants of Arabs, who had emigrated into that area from those very same regions, including present-day Syria, Egypt, Iraq, Jordan, and Saudi Arabia, during the previous century.

In 1950 Jordan annexed the West Bank. There were, to be sure, occasional calls in the ensuing years for the establishment of a Palestinian Arab state in that territory, but they received scant support in most Arab countries and were greeted with outright hostility by King Hussein, who considered it to be his own.

Since 1967 East Jerusalem and the West Bank have been Israel's in much the same way they were Abdullah's and Hussein's—by occupation. East Jerusalem, which now contains about 120,000 Arabs, has been annexed to Israel. The rest has been under Israeli administration.

Soon after the 1967 war many Israelis began arguing that the capture of the West Bank had brought under Israeli control the very heart of what they called Eretz Yisrael, or the Land of Israel. Much of the State of Israel that had been created in 1948 was located, they pointed out, in the segment of the Land of Israel that was least associated with Jewish history—the coastal plain, which was the home throughout much of the biblical era not of the Jews but of the Philistines. For the Jews the area that is now the West Bank was the center of their past and their identity. It was where the patriarchs spoke with their God and dug their wells. It was where the Jewish judges judged, the Jewish prophets prophesied, and the Jewish kings ruled. It was where the word of the Lord scorched Isaiah's tongue. Besides, Jews had maintained a persistent presence in what is now the West Bank, as well as in the rest of what was once their country, during the eighteen centuries since the Romans had renamed it Palestine, in memory of the Philistines, so as to banish forever the memory of Judea and its stubborn Jews. Despite the deaths of perhaps a million Jews in their rebellions against Rome and the dispersion of many more around the world, others remained in the land; still others returned to it. They were subjected to the repeated depredations of the many waves of conquerors, who in the best of times merely taxed and humiliated them and in the worst slaughtered them and drove them out. And among the places in which they hung on were such ancient towns as Hebron, holy to them whether ruled by Jews, Romans, Arabs, Crusaders, Egyptians, or Turks.

Despite this long and nearly unbroken Jewish presence in the part of Palestine that is now the West Bank, many Israelis were prepared after that territory came under Israeli control in 1967 to give it up, together with the Sinai and Gaza, in return for peace. But opposition to giving up the territory was powerful, stemming in the main from security concerns. Those concerns were felt with regard to the Sinai and Gaza, and with particular force with regard to the West Bank. That territory bulges into Israel in such a way that it leaves much of the Jewish state exquisitely vulnerable to military attack, particu-

larly its populous and narrow coastal strip, which in some spots
is only nine miles wide and could easily be overrun in a war.
These concerns about military vulnerability, along with the
Arab response to the war—which consisted not of a willingness
to trade peace for territory but of a firm refusal even to consider negotiations—were reflected in a policy, during the early and
middle seventies, of governmental inaction. Israel would wait
to find a negotiating partner in the Arab world, and meanwhile
nothing would be done in the West Bank that would unalterably change its character.

But things happened in the West Bank that did change its
character, and the Israelis who made them happen did so in the
hope that those changes would be permanent. Though Jewish
settlements were established in the West Bank during the first
decade after the 1967 war, primarily in the areas of greatest
military vulnerability, such as the Jordan Valley rift, the rate of
settlement increased markedly after 1977, when the Likud coalition was voted into power and Menachem Begin became
prime minister.

Followers of the teachings of Vladimir Jabotinsky—a Russian Zionist who believed that Jews had the right to a state in
their ancestral homeland, a state that should include the West
Bank—Begin and his colleagues set out to make the Jabotinsky
vision a reality. Surveys were done, and all land that had been
considered state property by the Jordanians prior to 1967 and
that had not been cultivated was declared suitable for Jewish
settlement. In addition Jews bought parcels of land from those
Arabs willing to sell them despite the death sentence that Jordan had promised to mete out to any Arab who did sell. On
occasion land that Arabs considered to be not state property
but their own was taken over by settlers. Sometimes Israeli
courts upheld the Arabs' objections; sometimes they did not.

By 1980 the character of the settlements had begun to
change. Though most of the early ones had been of the communal sort, many of them focusing on agriculture or light industry,
it was the urban developments that began to predominate, at
least in terms of population. No longer was arable land—nearly

all of it already spoken for by the Arabs—considered necessary. Bulldozers cleared hilltops that since the beginning of time had been shunned as sites of habitation, because the land could not be farmed, because water could not be found, and because they were hard to reach. Housing was installed at a remarkable pace. Private contractors were permitted to develop lots, and highly favorable mortgage terms were offered by the Israeli government. It became possible for a Jewish family to build a four-bedroom house in the West Bank, with a plot of land of its own, good schools, and stunning views, for the price of a small apartment in a crowded neighborhood in Tel Aviv—and within a twenty-minute commute from that city, and even closer to Jerusalem. According to Meron Benvenisti, a former deputy mayor of Jerusalem and a prominent Israeli opponent of the settlements policy, between 50,000 and 60,000 Jews from Tel Aviv alone may in the next few years move into the bedroom communities now being built on the neighboring West Bank hills.

But as effective as the Israeli government policies were in rapidly developing the West Bank settlements, it was the actions of the Gush Emunim that probably had the most effect in spurring the process. The members of this "Bloc of the Faithful"—made up mostly of native-born Israelis but also of immigrants from the United States and other countries—felt an obligation to resettle the Land of Israel.

That obligation was, for them, a holy one. As they saw it, the Six-Day War had been a kind of miracle. Surrounded by Arab countries that had sworn to erase Israel from the face of the earth—and to throw those Jews who survived the Arab onslaught into the sea—Israel nevertheless prevailed and even won the very territory that had been the birthplace of the Jewish people. Surely if God could do that much for his people, his people had the responsibility not to let the miracle pass away.

They wasted no time in fulfilling that responsibility. From the beginning they moved into places from which Jews had been expelled and in which they had been massacred. Some of those expulsions and massacres were the ancient ones of two millennia before; some were the more recent ones at the hands of the Arabs in the 1920s and 1930s. The Israeli government opposed such moves, particularly to highly populated Arab areas such as those in and around Hebron. But it was precisely such areas, with old Jewish roots, that most attracted the Gush Emunim. Sometimes the Israeli army was called out to extract these settlers. But eventually the settlements took hold and became the nuclei for permanent communities. And the people who had established the settlements, having fulfilled what they saw as a mitzvah, a holy commandment, moved on to establish still more settlements, always worried that a new Israeli government might come in — as one finally did in 1984 — that would be less partial to the goal of settling the West Bank than the Begin government was.

Begin proved himself very partial to that goal. His ultimate wish was the annexation of Judea and Samaria, the southern and northern parts of the West Bank, and he did what he could to guarantee that whatever political arrangements were finally made, Jews would always have the possibility of living in those areas.

In May of 1981, addressing 35,000 supporters rallying in the West Bank urban settlement of Ariel, Begin issued the kind of biblical declaration that had made him famous both in his native Poland and in Israel: "I, Menachem, the son of Ze'ev and Hana Begin, do solemnly swear that as long as I serve the nation as prime minister, we will not leave any part of Judea, Samaria, the Gaza strip, and the Golan Heights." In May of 1982 he insisted in the Knesset that in future negotiations on a peace treaty Israel would reject any proposal to dismantle any Jewish settlements. And four months later he rejected President Ronald Reagan's for an accommodation on the West Bank that included a freeze on the settlements. The American plan, he said, amounted to "the repartition of Eretz Yisrael." Harking back to Britain's assignment of the eastern part of Palestine to Abdullah, Begin declared, "If anyone wants to take Judea and Samaria from us, we will say, 'Judea and Samaria belong to the Jewish people to the end of time.'" And responding in the

Knesset to President Reagan's pledge to stick by his own proposals "with total dedication," even if Israel rejected them, Begin said, "The Israeli government rejected your proposals and
will stand by that with total dedication. But it's total dedication
with a difference. For you it's a matter of policy—to get closer
to Saudi Arabia or Hussein. For us it is our life, our homeland,
the land of our fathers and of our children."

Not that Begin, in saying that, was expressing the sentiments of all Israelis. Many, perhaps half, disagreed with the
goal of West Bank annexation, and a large percentage were
uncomfortable with the existence of the settlements. According
to recent polls even more are uncomfortable now.

To many Israelis the settlements policy has been too costly:
more than £1.1 billion, including £538 million for housing and
£58 million for roads, has been spent on the West Bank settlements in nonmilitary outlays by the government and the Jewish
Agency. At a time when Israel's foreign debt, now exceeding
£17 billion, is the highest per capita in the world and when its
inflation rate, once thought high at 200 percent, has already
reached a figure more than twice as high, many Israelis find
the continued investment of national funds in the settlements
an economically extravagant policy, no matter how con-
vincing the political, historical, religious, or security justifications may be. The economic concern becomes even greater
when it is realized that, to attain a population of 100,000 Jews
in the West Bank, it will be necessary to invest even more in
the area — according to Meron Benvenisti, about £1.9 billion
more. In 1984 it took a finance minister who was building
his own West Bank house, Yigal Cohen-Orgad, to propose
a severe cutback on funds for the construction of settlements,
including a freeze on the construction of many, if not all, of the
eighteen new ones planned for the year.

But by far the greatest opposition to the government's settlements policy comes from Israelis who fear its ultimate effects
on their country's social fabric, on its democratic principles,
and on its very purpose. Annexation would mean the incorporation of a very large number of Arabs into a country that was

founded as a Jewish state, an incorporation that is bound, they feel, to change the nation's character. And if the Arabs were not given full rights after such an incorporation, or if the current occupation merely continued without formal annexation, then Israel would be in the position of suppressing a large minority, denying them free expression, and keeping them subjugated by force, albeit force that is relatively mild by the usual standards of military occupation. This last prospect—the continued Israeli domination of an Arab population unwilling to be dominated—has been especially troublesome to many Israelis, who feel that the years of domination since 1967 have already changed Israel in very fundamental ways, forcing it to abandon some of its democratic precepts and causing it at times to behave toward Arabs in ways that other peoples, including Arabs, have often behaved, and sometimes still behave, toward Jews.

This concern has increased since 1980, as acts of Jewish vigilantism, carried out by a very small part of the settler population, have increased in frequency. Killings of settlers are sometimes followed by hand grenades thrown into Moslem schools and mosques; stones thrown at Israeli cars on West Bank roads, which sometimes result in crashes and deaths, often provoke drivers to emerge from their vehicles firing pistols and machine guns. Perhaps the most disturbing recent development has been the emergence and arrest, in 1984, of an underground settler group that planned and carried out a number of violent acts against Arabs, some of them against Arabs who were believed to have organized attacks on Jews and some of them against ordinary civilians, in retaliation for Arab attacks against Jews.

Israelis who have long prided themselves as members of a people who bear a legacy of culture, civilization, and social justice, and who have much to teach the world about the dangers of human violence because they have repeatedly witnessed it, cringe at such developments in their own country. Many are especially dismayed when they find themselves concluding that the justifications given for the violence by some of the settlers— that it is nothing but self-defense, that Jews must no longer sit

back and allow themselves to be butchered—makes at least
some sense and has at least a modicum of validity; and they are
discouraged, even shamed, by the realization that they have
become enmeshed in a reality in which acts they abhor make
any sense at all. They reject those acts and rail against the
reality that gives them their illusory necessity.

Israeli reservations about retaining the entire West Bank
began to grow after Menachem Begin resigned as prime minister
in September of 1983 and will probably continue to grow.
Without his powerfully focused vision of a Jewish return to the
Land of Israel, and without his voice to express that vision and
transmit its energy, it will be hard for any future Israeli leaders,
even if they are of his party and share his vision, to pursue it
with the same success and popular support that he did.

But the very existence of the settlements gives them a life
that propels them on. The process of settlement and de facto
annexation has gone on for so long, and has resulted in such
substantial changes, that it may be too late to reverse it.
Though deeply disturbed by the prospects that now face their
country and their society as a result of the settlements, the
Israelis who oppose them are startled by the changes that have
already taken place, that seem indelible, and that have frozen
many of them into resigned acquiescence.

It is unclear what effect the settlements have had on the
Palestinian Arabs—not only those in the West Bank but also
those who have been watching from afar, particularly members
of the Palestine Liberation Organization. To a great extent the
Israelis remained in the West Bank after the 1967 war because
no Arab country would negotiate with them. Now that parts of
the West Bank are moving under what seems to be permanent
Israeli control, one would imagine that at least some Palestinians, particularly those living in the West Bank, would be ready
to negotiate for their future while there is still a chance, and
would be ready, finally, to acknowledge Israel's right to exist.

It is the Arabs' refusal to grant this acknowledgment that,
the Jewish settlers have said, provides the political—as opposed
to the religious and the historical—justification, indeed

necessity, for Jewish presence in the West Bank. It isn't just the West Bank, they say, that the Palestinians want; they also want the rest of western Palestine, including Jaffa and Haifa. So why give them the means to finish the job? Why commit national suicide?

It was to understand these feelings and positions, and particularly their hold on the principal actors in the drama of the West Bank, that I recently visited the area. I wanted especially to understand the degree to which the settlers were committed to their vision, the ways in which the Arabs were responding to that vision, and the degree to which solutions of a political sort might still be possible. I visited and interviewed Jewish settlers as well as West Bank Palestinians, including leaders of both camps; and I interviewed Israelis who have sought ways other than West Bank settlement to fulfill the ideal of Jewish national expression.

The interviews were all carried out in English; some of the exchanges from them that are quoted here have been edited or condensed to increase clarity or eliminate repetitions or digressions. In the intensity of the clash between Arab and Jew I found sparks of searing light. Whether it was the light of God or Lucifer, or of some other realm, I cannot say; but it illuminated my quest, sometimes ignited it, and I present the images it left, as well as the embers, as faithfully as I know how.

2

The Arab Is a
Stranger in My House

More than anyone else, Rabbi Moshe Levinger has led and energized the Jewish settlement movement since it began. In 1968, less than a year after Israel won the Six-Day War, Levinger and a few other Jews moved into the Park Hotel in the West Bank city of Hebron and then refused to leave. That city, he insisted, was an ancient and holy Jewish town, a town in which Jews had lived almost continuously from biblical times, and one in which they had a right to live once again. After all, it contained the burial places of Abraham, Isaac, and Jacob; it was the place in which David was anointed King of Judah and then of Israel; and for the past 2,000 years it had been a seat of Jewish learning, despite repeated persecutions and expulsions of Jews by Arab Moslems, Christian Crusaders, Mamluks, and Ottomans. In 1929 local Arabs killed sixty-seven Jews and wounded another sixty, synagogues were burned, Jewish property was taken over, and the community was destroyed. The few Jews who returned were evacuated by the British in 1936 during another wave of anti-Jewish Arab rioting.

Levinger's sit-in at the Park Hotel was thus an attempt to reestablish, after a three-decade hiatus, the Hebron Jewish community. Despite complaints by Hebron Arabs and opposition from the Israeli government, Levinger, then thirty-three years old, stayed put. After six months in the hotel, he and his followers were given government protection at a nearby Israeli army camp. Finally, in 1970, the government gave in to Levinger's demand that he be permitted to build a Jewish settlement near Hebron. This was called Kiryat Arba—the name given in the book of Genesis as the original name of Hebron.

Not until 1974 was Gush Emunim—the movement dedicated to the Jewish settlement of the West Bank—founded, with Levinger its most visible and active leader. Its first official settlement, at Camp Horon, in Samaria, was established the day after Yitzhak Rabin became the Israeli prime minister, and many other settlements followed.

I visited Levinger in his home, next to the sixteenth-century Avraham Avinu Synagogue, which was plundered in the 1929 Arab rioting and rebuilt during the past few years. The synagogue and the house are located in a courtyard that was the center of Jewish life in Hebron for hundreds of years, in part because it was surrounded by tall buildings, which gave the Jewish community a measure of security during the Arab attacks to which it was subjected over the centuries. The buildings have crumbled over the centuries, and now security is provided by Israeli soldiers.

Levinger, who is tall and bearded, led me into the dining room of his three-bedroom apartment, where he lives with his American-born wife, Miriam, and seven of their eleven children, ages four to fifteen. Two of their children are married and live away from home; one studies in Jerusalem, nineteen miles to the north; and one, a married daughter, lives in Kiryat Arba, the Jewish settlement outside Hebron founded by her father. Of the children still living with the Levingers, the older ones attend school in Kiryat Arba and the younger attend kindergarten in Beit Romano, a large building adjoining the main market that had been an Arab girls' school before the settlers moved in. The settlers argue that the building is in fact the property of the Lubavitcher rabbi, who leads a Hasidic sect now centered in Brooklyn; the sect had bought property in Hebron in 1840 and had established a yeshiva there in 1900.

Levinger offered me a seat at the table where he and his

family eat and where he studies. The room, like the rest of the apartment, was austere, reflecting with fidelity the person of Levinger himself. Gaunt, careless of his appearance, wearing the coat of one suit and the trousers of another, he seemed unconcerned about anything but his mission to settle the Land of Israel—unconcerned about the small details of life, the accumulation of personal comforts, the distracting needs of self and family. In some ways otherworldly, in some ways the kind of revolutionary ascetic who moves peoples and nations, he seemed out of place, almost out of century, holding the cordless telephone that repeatedly interrupted our interview with its urgent messages.

The first Zionist, Levinger informed me, was not David Ben-Gurion and not even Theodor Herzl but God. It was the Land of Israel that God chose as his seat, as the place from which his moral teachings were to be issued, and it was the responsibility of the Jewish people to live in the land that God had given to them in order to live by his teachings and, in so doing, to enlighten the world. The honor of the world, he repeatedly insisted, was served by the Jews' return to their land—even the honor of the Arabs.

This religious mission has always been at the heart of Zionism, even the late-nineteenth-century political Zionism of Herzl, Levinger stressed. Herzl's Zionism, he argued, had attracted Europe's Jewish masses only because it touched something already deep in their hearts. Wasn't it, after all, for a return to Zion that they had been praying three times a day for two thousand years? Wasn't that hope contained in every one of their songs and rituals? Hadn't they always referred to themselves, in all the books written since they were expelled, as being *mihutz la'aretz*—"outside of the Land"? "In Poland," Levinger lectured, "the Jews were *mihutz la'aretz*. In Germany, *mihutz la'aretz*. In the Gemara [the portion of the Talmud written during the Babylonian exile], we say we are *mihutz la'aretz*. Always we knew we were outside of the Land. Which land? The land written in the Bible. And if there are now Arabs in that land, then they took it from the Jewish people! And they know it! They know it, but they say that God changed our status—that he abandoned us—and that we therefore don't have a country. But *we* say that God *didn't* change our status; we say that we were undeserving, that we behaved badly, that we didn't obey him, and that he therefore hid his face from us and punished us." Being "outside of the Land," Levinger summarized, was a temporary status that God had intended as a punishment for the Jews' transgressions. Now the Jews were back and were obliged to live in the land—all of the Land of Israel—as a worthy, holy and God-fearing people.

But, I pointed out, in returning to Judea and Samaria the Jews have come to a populated place—a place populated by Arabs who argue that the Jews have no right to settle among them. If not for the Israeli army guarding his home, I observed, he couldn't even be there.

Levinger was unperturbed. The Arabs, he argued, aren't just against the settlements in the West Bank. They're against Israel itself. They're against the very idea of Zionism, against the return of the Jews to their land of origin. To say that the Arabs are merely against the settlements is unrealistic, absurd: "Before the 1967 war, we had no settlements in Judea and Samaria, and they also wanted to destroy Israel. If we were to give up the settlements in the West Bank, then they would be against the settlements in Tel Aviv and Haifa and Netanya." The Arabs wouldn't be satisfied, Levinger insisted, until all Jews were out. And any suggestion the Arabs make that they *might* be willing to accept the borders of 1947, or of 1949, is a lie.

"But," I objected, "surely some compromise could be reached—"

Levinger grew irate. "You can compromise about unimportant things," he shot back, "but you can't divide your wife, you can't divide your children, you can't divide your Bible, and you can't divide your holy earth. And if a man is ready to divide his son, it means he doesn't believe that it *is* his son. To compromise on our own home, a home that belongs not only to us but also to God, is abnormal! You can't do it! It's the same as if you had a home and another man came in and said that a part belonged to him. You wouldn't compromise. You would fight until you possessed your beloved home. And all the more your beloved country!"

But that same country, I reminded Levinger, is also beloved by the Arabs; for them it's also home. Some of them have indicated a willingness, or at least a possible willingness, to accept Israel within its pre-1967 borders.

Levinger rejected the possibility that the Arabs would ever accept the Jews anywhere in the Land of Israel—either in the West Bank or within the pre-1967 borders. "It's a lie!" he insisted. "They don't want to compromise. It's only a pretense. They want it all! And," he added, "even if they wanted to compromise, *we* couldn't. If someone were to come to another person's house and want to take his house or sleep with his wife or take his children, he couldn't compromise on that!"

"But," I persisted, "what if the Arabs were really ready—"

"I've been explaining this to you for a quarter of an hour! If I wanted to take your wife from you, your children, you would accept that? You would say that because *I believe* it's right then it *is* right?" Levinger stared at me in amazement at the thought that anyone could compromise on his dearest possessions, on life itself. "If we believe that [this land] belongs to the Jewish people, then it's just abnormal for us to give it up. And if someone else comes and says it's his also, we should give him a part of it? Can you be serious?"

Repeatedly Levinger asked me, with incredulity, how I could expect him to leave his house, his home, just because someone else claimed it for his own. Repeatedly he placed me within the analogy to make it real: "If a man came into *your* apartment and sat down in it and said, 'I'm sitting here, so it belongs to me,' would that mean it's his? We were expelled from this land against our will, but we always knew that it was ours. We always knew, wherever we were, that we were in the *galut*—in the diaspora."

What, then, is to be done about the Arabs? I asked. After all, they form a majority of the population in the West Bank, and probably will for many years, perhaps forever, even if the

Jewish settlements continue to expand and proliferate.

The Arabs, Levinger answered, are welcome to live in Judea and Samaria in peace; they can control their own affairs and pursue their own lives. What they cannot do, he said, was to take the land away from the Jews. "It's our country," he insisted, "and it's our destiny to live in our land as a 'nation of priests.'" In principle, he added, "we invite the Arabs to live everywhere. But we don't believe they have the right to change the idea, the purpose, of the state. For that reason, I believe that they shouldn't be able to vote in national elections for the Knesset, because if they could then they would vote to change the purpose, the Jewish nature, of the state." Denying the Arabs the right to vote in Israeli national elections, Levinger admitted, rendered them in a sense second-class citizens. But, he added, if they were to dismantle the Jewish state by their vote, or change it into something other than a Jewish state, and in so doing take it away from the Jewish people and make it impossible for them to live as Jews in their own land, that would be a worse crime. It would be akin to the situation that would arise if a majority of Americans were to decide that they wanted to, say, legalize murder, and were ready to vote for that. Legalizing murder would destroy the foundation, the purpose, of American society, of democracy itself; and it would be correct to deny the majority the right to do that, to vote in that way, even though such a denial of the right to vote would compromise an important principle of American democracy. Similarly, denying Arabs the right to take the Land of Israel away from the Jews by voting it away from them—something that would happen if the Arabs, with their higher birthrate, were to become a majority in Israel—would be permissible, indeed necessary.

At the first of two meetings, which was held in Hebron, Levinger accepted my questions in the main with equanimity, even sufferance; he was used to interviewers, and seemed to feel an obligation to educate them about history. At our second meeting, however, held at the Gush Emunim headquarters, in Jerusalem, I realized that Levinger had decided not only to educate but also to convince me. It was here that I raised most of

my objections to his ideas, and here that he grew irritated, even
agitated, when I failed to accept his views and instead persisted
in questioning him about the rights of Arabs or about the possibility of territorial compromise. More than once he became
angry and scolded me for asking him to explain something so
simple as the idea that his land was his own, and that it represented, for him, something more than just property—that it
represented a holy place, a holy idea, a zone in which the Jews
were obligated to live a holy life that would serve to bring
honor to the world. And nothing, he repeatedly insisted to me,
could deter the Jews from fulfilling that obligation: "It's the
honor of the whole world that there is a Jewish state. And that
state can't be the state of both Israel and Ishmael, but of Israel
alone."

This Place Is in
My Genetic Code

Moshe Levinger's otherworldly, religious ideology contrasted sharply with the very practical, very secular vision of Elyakim Haetzni, another Jewish settler I interviewed.

Born in Germany in 1926, Haetzni emigrated to Israel twelve years later, not long before it became impossible for Jews to leave. He is in almost every way different from Levinger. He's a lawyer rather than a rabbi. He isn't religious. He speaks Arabic and counts many Arabs as his friends. He's lively, with a sharp and sarcastic sense of humor, and obviously enjoys sparring with people who disagree with him. But like Levinger, he's committed to the Jewish settlement of the West Bank.

However, he refuses to call it—and refused to allow *me* to call it—the West Bank. He insisted that I call the area Judea and Samaria: " 'The West Bank' is the term of my enemy. We are at war with Jordan; and 'the West Bank' is the linguistic embodiment of the Jordanian political claim to Judea and Samaria—it really means 'the West Bank of the Hashemite Kingdom.' So if you come to me and use the term 'the West Bank,' you really insult me. And I'm not ready to answer you if you use that term. So I'm sorry, you have no choice in the matter."

That's how Haetzni, in between spoonfuls of soup, began our interview, in the Savyon Restaurant, in West Jerusalem's genteel, quiet Jewish neighborhood of Rehavia, a few blocks from the homes of both Menachem Begin and his successor, Yitzhak Shamir. Haetzni was a member of the Council of Jewish Settlements and of the town council of Kiryat Arba. In 1972 he gave up a thriving legal practice in Tel Aviv and moved with his wife, three sons, and daughter to the hilltop outside Hebron that has since been their home.

I wasn't the first person forced to use Haetzni's terminology for the West Bank in order to be able to communicate with him. According to Haetzni, *Time* magazine used to send his subscription to "Kiryat Arba, West Bank." Haetzni complained to the *Time* office in Amsterdam, and they changed the subscription sticker to read, "Kiryat Arab, West Bank." "It must have been a Jew who did that," Haetzni laughed; "only a Jew could have contrived such a thing." He then wrote to Hedley Donovan, *Time*'s editor-in-chief, in New York, and asked him who had given the magazine the right to designate the name by which a country is called. "I threatened to sue him. Then I got a polite answer. They said it was a computer error. And since then I've been getting the magazine addressed to me at 'Kiryat Arba, Israel.'"

Whereas Levinger's English was halting, approximate, and indistinct, Haetzni's, though German-accented, was flowing and precise. And he needed almost no prodding from me to express his ideas.

"I started running in 1967," he told me, "and I've been running ever since."

"What started you running?"

"The Allon Plan."

The Allon Plan, named after the late Israeli foreign minister and deputy prime minister Yigal Allon, a member of the Labor Party, outlined several arrangements whereby Israel would retain parts of the West Bank for security purposes but would give up other parts, heavily populated by Arabs, which would be federated with Jordan. The main features of the plan involved the retention by Israel of the Jordan Valley rift and the Judean desert, as well as the easternmost ridge of the Samarian and Judean mountains, where military settlements and fortifications would be located. By this means, Allon and others believed, Israel would have some strategic depth in the West Bank, as well as a command of the heights overlooking the approaches that Arab armies would have to use to invade Israel from the east, while the Palestinians would be able to become part of a Jordanian–Palestinian state.

"It was a stunning surprise to me," Haetzni said, "when I learned that anyone could even dream of abandoning any part of the Land of Israel after waiting for it for 1,800 years. It's as if you're serenading your beloved beneath her balcony, and when she opens the window you go away! So I immediately began running to make sure that we wouldn't give up this land, and I haven't stopped running yet. You know, what makes me do all this running isn't my mind; it's my kishkes."

But Haetzni didn't seem satisfied that "kishkes" had conveyed how deep his attachment to the Land of Israel was. It was deeper, more primeval, than his guts. He told the story of a Palestinian Arab, "a hater of Zionism," who, after the establishment of Israel, in 1948, said that the Jews would never leave because the land was part of their heredity, part of their genes. "You know," Haetzni observed, "that Arab was a modern Bilam, the person in the Bible who blessed when he wanted to curse. He was absolutely right. This place is in my genetic code. It was my genetic code that cried out to live in this place.

"I came to this country from Nazi Germany in 1938, when I was twelve. I lived in Jerusalem, in Holon, in Ramat Gan. But I never felt as much at home as I did when I moved to Hebron. When I arrived there I felt that I had *returned*. That"—Haetzni emphasized, thumping the table between us—"is the land of the Bible."

Though Haetzni had admitted to me that he was not religious—certainly not religious in the way that Rabbi Levinger was—his attachment to the land clearly had roots in his Judaism. I asked him about those roots.

He answered with a question: "How can land be holy? After all, it's just earth—a chemical! I'll tell you how land can be holy. Eretz Yisrael is one of the central religious tenets in Judaism. Every Jewish prayer asks God to bring us back to Zion. Judaism and Zionism are simply inseparable. This is unique—only in Judaism is there such a phenomenon. We taught the whole world the notion that a land can be holy. Of course, whether we have the right to live here depends on *how* we live here. We are told that if we sin here, if we spill blood, we shall be kicked out. The land wasn't just given to us as an heirloom. Being here imposes more duties on us than rights."

I asked him whose blood he couldn't spill.

"Our blood, foreign blood, any blood. What's the difference between blood and blood? Is there a difference? People who see a difference are Nazis. Of course, I'm not talking about war. I'm talking about innocent blood."

I reminded Haetzni that just as there are Arabs who view Jews as being not quite as human as they, so there are Jews who view Arabs in much the same way.

"Jews who view Arabs in that way are beasts."

"Do you know any?"

"Yes."

"What do you say to them?"

"I say to them that if they adopt those views, that would give the Arabs the real victory over us."

Much more than Levinger, Haetzni was ready to talk about practical solutions. In fact, he had a very clear sense of how the central problem—the claims by two nationalities for the same land—could be resolved.

"It can be resolved by partition. The Arabs already have 78 percent of Palestine. But they prefer to call it Jordan in order to be able to demand the rest in the name of Palestine. Look, I'll tell you a story. In the beginning of the Lebanon War, in 1982, I went down to a garage in Hebron—an Arab garage. The owner is a friend of mine. His name is Abdul Jabbar; he calls himself Ovadiah, a Hebrew name. When he was an infant, he was given to a Jewish woman to be suckled, at a time when Jews were still living in Hebron. I said to Jabbar, 'What are the borders of Palestine?' And he answered, 'Palestine is the State

of Israel, the West Bank'—I'm using his term because I'm quot-
ing him—'the Gaza Strip, the Hashemite Kingdom of Jordan,
south Lebanon, Syria up to Damascus, and northern Sinai. This
is Palestine.' And I knew that he would answer that way; I hear
that answer from every Arab. So I said, 'Okay, you're right. But
this is also the Land of Israel. And so the translation of the
Land of Israel into Arabic is Palestine. So at least we're speaking about the same land.' Then I asked him, 'Tell me, how
many Israelis are there?' 'Three and a half million.' 'And how
many Palestinians?' 'Three and a half million.' 'So do you want
to partition it? How do you want to partition it? Lengthwise?
Crosswise?' I can tell you that if we had been given the eastern
part of Palestine in 1918 or 1920, it would have been the Garden of Eden by now, and in the western part there would have
been just rocks and deserts and swamps; and you would have
then said, 'The Jews, as always, took the better part!' That's
what I once heard from a British journalist who came for his
first visit to Israel from Jordan. He said, 'Small wonder the
Arabs are angry with you! You took everything that is green!'

"As you know, Winston Churchill arranged the first partition of Palestine, when he gave 78 percent of the area to the
Arabs. In fact, one of the Emir Abdullah's British advisers
openly said that this was done because ultimately the Jews
would set up a Jewish state and the British had to reserve a
place for the Palestinian Arabs who would want a state of their
own. Mind you, Jews owned land in the eastern part of Palestine and wanted to settle there; all of that was canceled in 1922.
And you should know Abdullah wanted to call Jordan by the
name Palestine, but the British told him not to do it; and had he
done so, America wouldn't have been able to say, 'The Palestinian Arabs have no homeland.'

"This is the tragedy: that at the very time the Jewish people
were being killed in Europe, including one and a half million
Jewish children, their own homeland was closed to them. Who
closed it? The Arabs—not without the help of the British, of
course, but mainly the Arabs. And the leader of the Arabs was
the Mufti of Jerusalem, Haj Amin al-Husseini, who was in the

entourage of Hitler. He even went to Auschwitz to see it. And toward the end of the war, when a few SS leaders wanted to save a few hundred Jewish children in order to establish an alibi for themselves, the Mufti went to Hitler and prevented it, because he wanted to burn the Jews there in Europe so that they wouldn't come here.

"So this was the first demographic change that affected the question of Palestine: the destruction of Europe's Jews, including those who, had they lived, would have come here. The second demographic change occurred because of the Arab refusal to accept the UN resolution in 1947 creating a *second* Palestinian state. Because of this there was a war, a refugee problem, and now the Palestinians from western Palestine make up the majority of the population of Jordan—between 60 and 70 percent.

"I had a British woman reporter visit me who was very nasty—polite, but nasty. So I wanted to be nasty, also. So I said to her: 'You remember the man who jumped the fence to your queen and found her awake because she couldn't sleep? Do you know what they talked about? I'll tell you. The man said, "My gracious Queen, why are you so sleepless?" And the queen answered, "Because of the Palestinian problem." Over what do people lose sleep these days? Over the Palestinian problem! Well, the man didn't know what to answer her. He should have answered, "Over *which* Palestinian problem? The Palestinian problem in *western* Palestine or the Palestinian problem in *eastern* Palestine?" The Palestinian problem in western Palestine is the problem of a *third* of the population—the Palestinian Arabs of what you call the West Bank, of Gaza, and of pre-1967 Israel ‹ make up a third of the population of that area—while the Palestinian problem in eastern Palestine is the problem of the majority, of *two thirds* of the population in Jordan. So where should you seek their self-determination? Where they are a minority or where they are a majority? So,' I said to that British reporter, 'the next time you talk to your queen, tell her over what she should be losing her sleep. And ask her why she doesn't lose sleep over the Kurds. Or over the Arabs in Khuzistan, which is called Arabistan. Or over the Germans in the places where they are dominated by other countries. Or over the Corsicans, the Basques, the Copts—the whole world! But it's only over the Palestinians that she loses sleep. So if she loses sleep over them, then at least she should lose sleep over the Palestinians in eastern Palestine, in Jordan, where they form a majority and still have no state!'"

Haetzni was once described to me as "a crazy" by an American journalist who had interviewed him, and this story shows why. Haetzni was describing to me, with great satisfaction, how he had disarmed and confused a hostile British journalist with an invented story about her own queen, and how he had used the invention, apparently accepted as real by that stunned journalist, at least momentarily, in order to get her to listen to what he had to say—and in order to tweak her unsympathetic British nose. My friend the American journalist was, I knew, no less hostile to Haetzni's beliefs; and I suspect that in his talks with the American Haetzni had used whatever stratagem he could devise to tweak *his* nose—which was, no doubt, all the more worthy of tweaking, since it was the nose of a Jew, who, Haetzni must have felt, should have known better.

Perhaps deciding that I might begin to think that my own nose was being tweaked and that all of his stories were inventions and all of his statements merely sarcastic asides, Haetzni quickly grew serious. "I sincerely do feel," he went on, "that the Palestinian Arabs have developed the traits of a nation. Of course we shouldn't overdo it the way Mr. McGovern did when he came here and spoke of the thousands-of-years-old culture of the Palestinians. Because the Palestinian Arabs first developed a feeling that they were a nation in the 1920s—imitating Zionism. This is not something for us to be ashamed of; our movement, Zionism, gave birth to two nationalisms—Jewish nationalism and Palestinian nationalism. So it's our responsibility that there's a Palestinian nationalism. And what we should do now is foster a Palestinian nation, a Palestinian state in Jordan."

To Haetzni, the creation of such a state is crucial. "There

should be a strong, free Palestine on the East Bank of the Jordan—in alliance with us, maybe in a federation. We should annex Judea, Samaria, and Gaza. There should be complete autonomy in those places for the Arabs—Jordanian law, or some other Arab law, should prevail, and this should be legislated by the Knesset. This would be genuine autonomy—in the health system, in local government, and in anything else that doesn't have to do with the superstructure of the state, security, and foreign relations. And the Arabs can have a Palestinian state on the other side of the Jordan. Instead of having Jordanian passports, the Arabs in the annexed territories on this side of the Jordan would have Palestinian passports issued by the Palestinian state on the East Bank. Today they are eligible to vote in Amman, to the extent that _any_ Jordanians are allowed to vote; and under my plan, that eligibility would continue, except that they would be voting in the Palestinian state. And, I should add, just as Arabs would be permitted to live in Judea and Samaria, in the Jewish state, so Jews should be permitted to live in the Palestinian state, on the eastern side of the Jordan River; and those Jews would, of course, vote in Israeli elections, not Palestinian ones. And there should be open bridges between the two states. There should be a Law of Return for the Arabs. If an Arab wants to buy a house and live in Jaffa, why not?"

"But," I objected, "what if that Arab says, 'It was my house, and I want it back'?"

"No, no, no. That house has changed hands twenty times. If a German were to come to Kaliningrad and say, 'This city was once Koenigsberg, and this is my house,' the Russians would answer him, on the train ride to Siberia, 'Don't you remember that there was a war? That we paid with twenty million dead?' Where in the world did you ever see the clock turned back in a case in which one side was vanquished? But a war in which Jews win seems to be considered differently."

Haetzni was now on a topic—the world's hypocrisy—that clearly had exercised him in the past and that continued to do so in that restaurant.

"Look, UN Resolution 242—which says that acquisition of

land by war is forbidden—is the biggest lie since Cain and
Abel. And all the nations who signed it are liars. Take America.
America should give back New Mexico and California. They
can keep Alaska and Louisiana, because they purchased them.
All the rest should be given back. And take the other signers—
all of them took land and kept it. But *we* can't. So this Resolution 242 is like a Jewish yellow star in international law. It's a
shame! It's a lie! And the question you asked me about Arabs
moving back into the houses they abandoned in 1948 is a 242
question—it's based on a lie. The question isn't why we don't
give back the Arabs their old houses. The question is, why
haven't we paid them reparations for the property we took? If
we had done so, we would have reprieved the honor of the
Arabs. That would go a long way toward peace."

Under Haetzni's plan the Arabs of the annexed West Bank,
in being denied the right to vote in Israeli elections, would be
treated differently from the Arabs within Israel's pre-1967 borders, though the status of Judea and Samaria would otherwise
be the same as that of the rest of Israel. I asked him why. His
answer was based simply on numbers: the Arabs of Judea, Samaria, and Gaza, together with those of the Galilee, the part of
pre-1967 Israel that is about 50 percent Arab, would make up
33 percent of the population of Israel; and a 33 percent Arab
vote in the Knesset would result in a binational state. Eventually the Arabs, because of their higher birthrate, might be able to
muster enough votes to change the laws so that Israel would no
longer serve as the Jewish homeland—the place where Jews
being hounded elsewhere can come and receive refuge and
automatic citizenship.

To Haetzni, this strange plan—the creation of an area that
would belong to one state but most of whose citizens would
vote in another—was not strange at all. "Take the hundred
thousand or so Arabs in East Jerusalem," he explained. "East
Jerusalem has been annexed to Israel, and those Arabs now
have the choice of taking Israeli citizenship. But very few have
done so. [According to recent Israeli government statistics, of
the approximately 120,000 Arabs in East Jerusalem only 300

have so far accepted Israeli citizenship.] And you can't blame them. They would be choosing citizenship in a state whose national anthem speaks about the Jewish soul! Look, you Americans are trying to impose European notions on the Middle East, and you'll succeed as much as you succeeded when you tried to impose democracy on the Diem regime in South Vietnam. It's so foolish to impose such notions here. Are there any democratic countries among the Arab states? Was anybody elected in those countries? Sadat? Mubarak? Assad? Democratic notions are simply irrelevant in this part of the world. The best we can do is turn to our Arab neighbors and say, 'We recognize that this is your country and your homeland; you're attached to it with the same feelings that we are. You can stay here for as long as you like—for the next five thousand years. You can have all the civil rights that are possible—habeas corpus, freedom of speech; the only free Arab press in the Middle East is right here in Jerusalem. What we can't give you are political rights. Those rights you should seek in the 78 percent of Palestine that is under Jordanian sovereignty. If you want to change that sovereignty, and make it Palestinian sovereignty, we shall help you.'

"I think that ultimately this will be the solution. For me there is no difference where a Palestinian lives. If a Palestinian living in Brazil wants to return, and buys a home in Jaffa, maybe with reparations that I pay him, and he doesn't vote in the Knesset—what would be the problem? We don't have racial feelings toward them. The problem is *political*—it's not on a human level. This problem of voting is, practically speaking, irrelevant in the Middle East. In which Arab country do people vote? So here, if people voted in the elections of a country in which they don't live, it would be a precedent. What's wrong with a precedent? On the contrary: it would give professors of international law something to talk about!"

I asked Haetzni if an arrangement of this sort existed anywhere. He wasn't sure. "But," he said, "even if there were absolutely no precedent, even if it would be absolutely unique, that would be even better. What's wrong if the problem here is a unique one and has a unique solution? In fact, the problem here really *is* unique. Israeli nationality has something to do with Jewishness, and we don't have the urge to force people to accept Jewishness. And the Arabs for their part have their own rich cultural heritage and are in the midst of a period in which they're fervently nationalistic. Besides, they have a language that is ten times richer than Hebrew. So there's no urge by masses of Arabs to become like Jews. So neither side has an urge to incorporate the other.

"But there's another way in which the problem is unique here, and therefore requires a unique solution. Let me tell you a story. Once when my wife was buying grapes in Hebron—we have beautiful grapes in Hebron—an Arab woman asked her, 'Why did you come here? We were here *before* you.' And my wife had the presence of mind to answer, 'And we were here before *you*.' In other words"—Haetzni beamed—"if having been somewhere *before* is an argument, then we have a super-argument, because we were here *before* the before.

"Now, such an argument is available only to the Jewish people. If the Etruscans were to be discovered living somewhere in Africa and they were to return to Florence, then they would have such an argument too. But they're safely tucked away in the museums.

"Sometimes I try to explain to Palestinians what happened to them. I tell them a story: An Iraqi Arab, a Syrian Arab, and a Palestinian Arab were walking on the street, and a brick fell from a roof. On whose head did it fall? On *your* head—on the head of the Palestinian. The name of the brick is the Jewish fate. If the descendants of Nebuchadnezzar were alive today, then the Iraqis would have a problem. But it's the Palestinians who have that problem.

"Now, there is only one such brick. There is no other people alive today with the conscious sense that they are the direct descendants of people from the ancient world. The Colosseum stands intact in Rome, but the people in that city don't have the feeling that they are the descendants of the ancient Romans. But if you go to Masada, you read the inscription 'Masada Will

Not Fall Again!'—as if it fell just yesterday. And for us the Wailing Wall is contemporary, not classical, history. This is unique. When we have a question about contemporary Jewish ritual, we check the archaeological digs and get the answers. If we don't know something about the correct size of a ritual bath, for example, we measure the remains of the ritual bath on Masada. So we have bridged time, as if the gap in time between our period of sovereignty here before the expulsion and our current period of sovereignty didn't exist. It's as if we had a time machine. *Nu*, there is no other nation of this kind! And this is the unique problem that befell the Palestinian Arabs.

"But you have to add to this the fact that the Palestinian Arabs weren't here for such a long time. Most of them came here during the past hundred to a hundred and fifty years. Before that the country was completely depopulated. And you can immediately tell from where they are. Yesterday I got four new clients from Yatta. The Israeli authorities found arms in their houses. They're not from Fatah [a PLO organization]— Fatah clients I don't take. Yatta is wild country, like the Shouf Mountains in Lebanon, full of feuds; it's just south of Hebron."

I had assumed that all of Haetzni's clients were Jews; I was surprised to learn that Arabs turned to him for his services, but he insisted that many of his clients were indeed local Arabs. "Why don't they go to Arab lawyers?" I asked. "Because," he said, laughing, "they don't trust them!"

Haetzni returned to the subject of his new clients. One had said his name was Masaruwa. The name Masaruwa, Haetzni explained to me triumphantly, was the name of someone whose family had come from Egypt. "When did his family come from Egypt? Who knows? A hundred and fifty years ago. At the most two hundred years ago. Look, there's a very big town in Judea called Dura. Two hundred years ago two tribes from Saudi Arabia came there and killed off all the people of Dura, then killed off each other—from the second tribe only a fifth remained—and this is Dura! And they have taken the whole range of the Hebron Mountains from Dura to the south. And they know it!

"Sometimes they're so conscious of it. There is a town called Dhahiriya. Three Arabs were sitting there talking, and one says, 'Our great-grandfather came from Saudi Arabia.' And then one of them kicks him. Why? Because they don't want to upset the myth that they are the ancient inhabitants of Palestine, from time immemorial, and we, the Jews, are the newcomers."

Haetzni said that he doubted that the Palestinian Arabs would ever give up on their wish to take back Jaffa or Haifa. But he insisted that neither that lingering wish nor the disinclination of Arab states to make peace with Israel would stand in the way of the political solution he had outlined to me. This solution, he asserted, is advantageous to both Israelis and Palestinians. The Palestinians, he said, know that only the Israelis could see to it that they would have their own state—a state in what is now Jordan. King Hussein, they know, wouldn't give them a state and didn't do so when he controlled Judea and Samaria. So the Palestinians secretly know that their only chance for political independence is some kind of accommodation with Israel. And as for the Israelis, it's more important for them to do what they can to achieve some kind of accommodation, even federation, with a Palestinian state on the East Bank of the Jordan than it is to achieve peace with other Arab states. On the matter of returning any part of Judea and Samaria, Haetzni was adamant. "If we ever give them Hebron, they'll still want Jaffa and Haifa. They won't give up on that no matter what we do. So it won't help."

Haetzni seemed absolutely certain of the path he had chosen when he moved to the West Bank. "Do I have any alternative? What would I say to my Maker if I had this opportunity and didn't use it? What would I say if I had this opportunity to return to my homeland and didn't take it? It would be a sacrilege. It would be an outrage. It would be a shame. And it would be a tragedy."

So Let the Arabs Vote—
I'm Not Afraid

For Yisrael Medad, the main fear of both Levinger and Haetzni—the fear that if the Arabs in an Israeli-annexed West Bank were allowed full political rights in Israel, including the right to vote, they could vote out the Jewish state—did not exist.

Medad is a thirty-seven-year-old Bronx-born Israeli who lives in the West Bank settlement of Shiloh with his wife and five children. For ten years he has been working for Geula Cohen, a member of the Knesset representing the right-of-center Tehiya, or Renaissance, Party; he has worked as a teacher in Cohen's educational institute and as her parliamentary aide. As a former American he understands, much better than Levinger does, Western, particularly American, sensibilities about the issue of Arab rights; and it's to him that visitors are often referred when they come to complain about that issue.

In Medad's view, Arabs should be offered full political rights in an annexed West Bank, including the right to vote in national elections for the Knesset. And Medad is unafraid that that right would, because of the Arabs' high birthrate, eventually give them the votes to dismantle the Jewish state.

He doesn't fear that because, he explained, he supports a plan that would allow the Arabs to become voting citizens of the Jewish state only if they first accepted the principle that the

33

state was, by its definition, unalterably Jewish—that it wasn't just another state, like all the other states of the world, but rather in perpetuity the Jewish homeland, the place to which any Jew can return. The Arabs would also have to be willing to participate fully in Israeli society, a participation that would involve the responsibility to defend the state. Medad acknowledged that Arabs could not be expected to fight in the Israeli military against other Arabs; consequently they would be expected to do alternative national service, but for a length of time equal to that put in by Jewish Israelis.

If they accepted these conditions for Israeli citizenship, Medad said, Arabs would no longer be a threat to Israel, even if their population increased to such an extent as to enable them to elect 61 members in the 120-member Knesset; after all, under his plan it would be illegal for even a majority to change the Jewish purpose of the state. Moreover, Medad doubted that all Arabs would accept his conditions; some would, but probably most would not, preferring to keep their Jordanian—or perhaps Palestinian—citizenship and vote in the state, whether it was called Jordan or Palestine, that was located on the East Bank of the Jordan River. The likelihood that most Arabs would exercise the latter preference makes Medad confident that the offer of full political rights in Israel would not endanger the state or its purpose.

This plan—the plan of the Tehiya Party—would be acceptable to 80 percent of the Jewish settlers on the West Bank, in Medad's estimation; the settlers did *not* want an apartheid-like state. The accusation that they did, Medad insisted, was wrong: "I want Arabs to be integrated into Israeli society and do things that Jews do, such as national service. Besides, I resent this comparison of the position of the Jews in Israel with the position of the whites in South Africa. The white settlement in South Africa was started by a bunch of Dutch people who came into the region a couple of hundred years ago, people who had never been there before and whose ancestors had nothing to do with that land. Here, the Jews returned to their land."

Medad acknowledged that under this plan one part of the

West Bank population—Arabs—would not be able to exercise all of the rights that persons accustomed to Western democratic practices ordinarily assume belong to all peoples. That is, even those who chose Israeli citizenship would be unable, no matter how numerous they were, to change Israel from a Jewish state into an Arab one; and those who chose not to accept Israeli citizenship would have no say in matters affecting the country as a whole.

But such limitations on political rights would not really be so odd, even from a Western democratic perspective, Medad argued. All that the Arabs would lack would be the right to sovereignty. "But who says that every people has the right to sovereignty—the right to dominate others—wherever they live? Let's take the Jews of Brooklyn. If they constituted 40 percent of the population and had lived there for three hundred and fifty years, that wouldn't give them the right to secede from the United States. There are certain limitations on the freedoms of national groups."

Medad echoed a point made by Elyakim Haetzni: the situation in the West Bank is simply different from any other and requires a different solution. "I agree with you that it sounds silly for a bunch of Jews whose parents came from Russia, Poland, and Germany, and who themselves came from America, France, and England, to come into an area that was populated by other people and claim that it's their home. But it *is* their home. It's a unique situation. And any outsider coming in to try to solve the situation is confronted by something very difficult. What that person then tries to do, what he tries to offer as a solution, reflects his own experience, the experience of the situations in the rest of the world, which are very different, and which don't apply to this situation here, a situation which is very unique, and which has become a problem because of its unique nature—because it involves the return to a land of a people that was expelled from it but that kept its memory and reality alive every day for two thousand years."

Medad went on to justify the definition of the West Bank as Jewish on yet other grounds. The Jews, he said, had proved that

the land was theirs by the way they lived on it. They loved it.
They were tender toward it. They caressed it. They cultivated it.
They planted in it. And the land in turn gave them its fruits.
What had the Arabs done for the land? What kind of lovers
were they? They neglected it. Their allegiance was to the village
rather than to the land. And if they had finally developed a
Palestinian nationalism, they had done so only after having
been confronted by the nationalism of the Jews. Before that
they had been just Arabs living in villages, often migrants from
nearby areas such as Egypt, Arabia, Syria, Iraq, or Turkey; and
if they felt themselves to be part of anything larger than the
village they happened to live in, it was perhaps the Arab nation,
not the Palestinian people. For them the land was incidental; it
was where their village happened to be. Besides, Medad added,
during the 1948–1949 Arab–Israeli war the Arabs ran away
too easily, much as the Jews used to run away from towns in
Poland and the Ukraine when hostilities would start in those
regions; the Arabs ran because they weren't committed to the
land, whereas the Jews in the Land of Israel, even during war,
would never leave it.

I quickly objected to these arguments. Different peoples
lived differently in their lands and possessed those lands in different ways, I said; making the desert bloom, or draining
swamps, did not by itself establish ownership. Nor did readiness to flee prove the transience of ownership: in wars people
flee. But Medad's arguments were, by the time I heard them,
fixed stars in the Gush Emunim ideological firmament—not
central, but still important. And my objections failed to dislodge them in the least.

Against Medad's central arguments, too, I was able to muster few of my own that convinced him. My American inclina-
tion to challenge him on the grounds of Arab rights was met by
his repeated reminders that, while the issue for the Arabs was
one of rights, the issues for the Jews, and for Israel, was one of
existence. "You have to understand," he lectured me patiently,
"that you're looking at the problem from an American perspective. What are Americans acquainted with? They're acquainted,

for example, with the problem of American blacks insisting on civil rights. But the problem of the blacks in America is different from the problem of the Arabs in Israel. Blacks in America never wanted to deny nationhood to the whites, while Arabs here do want to deny nationhood to the Jews. There's a fundamental difference. I have very strong reasons to believe that no matter what we do the Arabs will never be satisfied. If we say to the Palestinians that they're welcome to have the West Bank, that wouldn't satisfy them, either; they would want the rest of our land, they would want pre-'67 Israel. And all we would accomplish by giving back these territories would be to increase our level of danger. And I genuinely believe that if we lived under Arab rule the situation for us would be much, much worse than the situation is for Arabs under Israeli rule. It would be a question of our very survival. We would be killed. It would be Hebron, 1929; it would be Kfar Etzion, 1948."

Just Wait Till
We Have the Power

When the Arab taxi dispatcher at Jerusalem's Damascus Gate learned that I would be writing something about the West Bank, he insisted that I include his story. He had been imprisoned by the Israelis, he said, for fifteen years.

"Fifteen years! Fifteen years of my life!"

I asked him why.

"Because the Israelis said I was PLO. They said I was a terrorist."

"Were you?"

The dispatcher was taken aback. I continued: "What did they say you did?"

"They said I planted a bomb."

"Did you?"

"I did."

"Where?"

"In a movie theater."

"What happened?"

"Somebody found it and took it outside. It exploded outside."

"Why did you do it?"

"I was protesting the immigration of Jews."

The dispatcher finally found a taxi driver willing to take us—a young Arab journalist and me—to Hebron. We set off to the south, and I asked the journalist, who had himself spent time in an Israeli jail, what he thought of the story.

"Fifteen years is a large part of one's life," he observed.

"But what about the bomb?"

"Well, it didn't kill anyone."

"But wasn't he a terrorist?"

"He was fighting for what he believed in."

"But what if the bomb had gone off inside the theater? What if that theater had been filled not with Israelis but with Arabs—with your brother or your father?"

We drove on to Hebron in silence.

———————

Mustafa Natshe was waiting for me in the foyer of his spacious, even lavish, house. Some days before, while driving me around the West Bank, a Gush Emunim settler had told me that very few Jews in Israel lived as opulently as did many of the Arabs in the West Bank. "It's money from the Gulf," he explained. Without doubt, many of the houses lining the main roads north and south of Jerusalem were opulent indeed. "They look like apartment houses, don't they?" the settler asked. I agreed. "Well, they're not. They're houses built by wealthy Palestinians for their families. Some of them have maybe thirty rooms, and four or five floors, each floor for a different part of the family. Maybe a son and his family on one floor, a daughter and her family on another. I've been in some of those houses, I've been invited into them, and what's amazing is that they're empty. Really, they're empty. You'd be surprised. There's some furniture, but not much else. You'd expect oriental carpets, elaborate things. But mostly they're empty. I really don't understand it. And I really don't understand their taste, either. Look at those Eiffel Towers on the roofs." Nearly every roof did in fact have a not-so-miniature Eiffel Tower serving as a television antenna. The settler's offended aesthetic sensibilities, expressed as much with puzzlement as with dismay, reminded me of the offended sensibilities of West Bank Arabs who had told me more than once that they could not understand how the Jews could violate their pristine hilltops, barren for centuries, with the instant and crude habitations that belonged more in the vulgar suburbs of America than in the ancient landscapes of the Middle East.

Mustafa Natshe's house, in Hebron, was not so opulent on the outside as some of the million-dollar houses along the Jerusalem–Ramallah road, but inside it was more lavishly appointed than the ones the settler had described. Natshe, a heavy-set man of fifty-three, dressed on that warm night in a pin-striped suit, invited me into his living room. The evening prayers from the mosque, in this, the most religious and conservative of the West Bank towns, a community of 70,000 with no cinemas or places of entertainment, floated through the open window. A series of red velvet sofas was arranged around the room, with gold velvet drapes along the walls. Lace doilies adorned the sofas, a blue rug the floor. I felt too informal in my shirt-sleeves.

Natshe, formerly the acting mayor of Hebron, had recently been dismissed by Israeli authorities; so had his city council. The dismissals had occurred shortly after Aharon Gross, a nineteen-year-old Jewish seminary student, had been stabbed to death in the town's vegetable market. Gross was the eighth Jew killed in Hebron in three years, and his murder followed a number of other anti-Jewish incidents there, most of them involving stones or grenades thrown at Israeli cars.

After the killing, Jews from nearby Kiryat Arba descended on the vegetable market and set fire to most of its stalls. Israeli authorities, perhaps to assuage the settlers' anger, then dismissed Natshe, whom the settlers regarded as a fomenter of anti-Jewish violence. Miriam Levinger, the American-born wife of Rabbi Moshe Levinger, remarked to a reporter a few days after the burning of the vegetable market: "The Arabs take a life for a life. I say the Jews deserve credit for not killing any Arabs." Within days Hebron's Islamic University was attacked. Three Arabs were killed and thirty-three wounded.

Natshe explained to me that for a long time before his dismissal the Jewish settlers had been harassing and even terrorizing Hebron's Arabs. In October of 1982, he said, they had placed booby-trapped grenades in an Arab area. Then, he added, they had demolished five Arab houses for the purpose of building twenty-two apartments for Jews; the houses, they insisted, were located on property that had been owned by Jews before they were killed or forced to leave in 1929. Natshe went to the Israeli Supreme Court and obtained an injunction against that plan. Then, Natshe said, the settlers placed a grenade in a mosque; two people, he went on, were injured. "And they created other harassments. In June of 1983 they claimed that a grenade was thrown into the building they call Beit Romano; and after that our central market and bus station"—both of which stood on land that, the settlers argued, had once been Jewish—"were closed. The settlers then went to the military governor's office and asked that the city council and I be dismissed. This is not the first time that they did that. A year ago they demanded it as well. They said that I had an anti-Israel poster in my office. That poster had been placed in my office by the nationalist societies of Hebron. They also said that I didn't supply them with water. They made many claims against me."

I asked Natshe if any of the claims against him were correct.

"They *weren't* correct. They just wanted to get a city council that would be blind to their harassments. Because we used to go to the Israeli Supreme Court in Jerusalem and stop their actions."

Why would he go to the Israeli Supreme Court? Did he have faith in the Israeli courts?

"Yes, you can get justice from the Supreme Court. You can't get justice from the military administration. And the reason the settlers didn't like us was that we would go to the Supreme Court. . . . We sent a cable to the defense minister warning him that the settlers were about to carry out several provocations to try to show that we were a hotbed of criminal activities. When the settler, Aharon Gross, was stabbed in the city, we condemned the act. And we have doubts about who did it. After all, who gets the benefit from this? Only the settlers!"

Natshe had been acting mayor of Hebron since May of 1980, when Fahd Kawasmeh, the mayor, was deported, together with other Arabs, including Mohammed Milhem, the mayor of Halhul. Natshe explained that he had refused to assume the title of mayor because to do so would have been to recognize the dismissal of Kawasmeh as a legal act.

Natshe said that he had never had any contact with the Jews of Kiryat Arba, despite the proximity of that Jewish settlement. "No, never. Because I didn't want it. Because we believe that the Jewish settlements in the occupied areas are illegal. Settlements would be legal only if there were a comprehensive solution to the Palestinian problem. When the Arabs have their rights, when all the problems are solved, why not? An Arab will have the right to return to Jaffa and Lod and Ramla, and the Jew who wishes to return to settle in this city, why not?" Apparently, Natshe felt that the Jews who might be permitted to settle in the West Bank Palestinian state once it was established would be those who were literally returning—that is, Jews who had lived in the area of the West Bank prior to the establishment of Israel, in 1948, and perhaps the descendants of Jews who were killed in various massacres there. "But who," Natshe asked, "has come to settle here? They are not the Jews who lived here until 1929. They are fanatics coming from the States. They say that we must be expelled to the other part of the Land of Israel, which is Jordan. But we say no. We say there are two nations here, the Arab and the Israeli. We must have an independent state as Israel has a state. We must not be governed by the Israelis."

Which borders, I asked Natshe, would his envisioned Palestinian state have?

"The borders according to the UN partition plan of 1947."

"Oh," I responded, "you want to go back to the partition before the 1948 war."

"Yes. Before the war. The UN partition plan of 1947 gives the Arabs and the Israelis the right to have their own states. This is the basis on which negotiations must begin."

"In 1947," I began, "there was a partition plan in which a small area was to be given to Israel—"

"Not small."

"Smaller than the area Israel had after the Arab–Israeli war of 1948."

"Yes, of course. Smaller, but not much smaller. And this is the base from which we must start negotiations for Israel to be created in the area and also for the Palestinian state to be created."

"But Israel already exists. And the 1967 borders appear to be the minimal reality—"

"I didn't say this or that. I just say that this is the base from which negotiations must begin!"

"So you recognize the Israeli state."

"Yes."

"Unlike the PLO, which does not recognize it."

"Yes."

"Except that you say that the Israel you recognize is the state within the 1947 partition boundaries, not the state within the armistice lines after the 1948–1949 Arab–Israeli war."

"Yes."

"Now Israel is currently in the position, as a result of the 1967 war, of being internally torn between those Israelis who are willing to give up the West Bank for the sake of peace and those Israelis who proclaim it to be the central part of the Land of Israel and wish to hold on to it, as exemplified by the settlers and to some extent by the government. When those Israelis who are willing to give up the West Bank explain their position to those who are not, the answer they get is 'Don't be silly. We'll give up the West Bank and then they'll want the rest of Palestine. After all, the PLO still hasn't accepted the existence of Israel.' If you, Mayor Natshe, as a responsible representative of the West Bank Palestinian people, say that even *you* don't accept Israel's pre-1967 borders, aren't you encouraging that response?"

Natshe seemed irritated by my question. "Look, the most

important question is whether the Israeli government recognizes our right to self-determination. Why do we argue about borders if we still haven't gotten recognition of our rights?"

But I continued to argue, and in my arguing I felt as I had two days earlier, when I had argued with Natshe's neighbor Rabbi Moshe Levinger: I felt that the person I was facing couldn't understand how his interviewer could be so foolish. "But by the same token," I said, "it could be argued that if borders aren't so important, why don't you accept Israel within its 1967 borders?"

Natshe's irritation grew. "Look, *who* doesn't accept? If I said that the 1967 borders are okay, would the Israeli government accept the Palestinian state?"

In fact, Natshe seemed more moderate in his outlook than I had been led to believe by his enemies in the Gush Emunim: he was willing to state publicly that he could accept Israel—a rump Israel but an Israel nevertheless. That was further than I would have thought he would be willing to go, and further than PLO leaders had ever gone—save a few, such as Issam Sartawi, who had been assassinated in April of 1983 for being too moderate.

A young boy served us tea. I began to talk to Natshe as if what we said would make a difference, as if reasoning could change things. "The subject we're dealing with is very complicated," I said unnecessarily. "The Arabs feel that this is their land, that it has been taken from them. Some Jews feel that there is a place here for Jews as well—that they have a historic claim here. And so there is a clash of two nationalities. Can this clash, Mayor Natshe, be resolved?"

"It can be," Natshe answered, "if the Israelis really want peace. Let's start with 1947. After the Israelis got the land, they took another step. They got more land. Then, in 1967, they took yet another step. They got still more land. So you find that the Israelis kept on getting more and more land, because they had power. They rely on power. In Lebanon, I'm sure, if they didn't have problems, they would have never withdrawn, even from Beirut. They want to keep southern Lebanon. They want to keep the Golan Heights. The next step will be to enter Jordan and take the heights of Irbid. We see that the extremists are planning these things, and that all the people are involved in this planning. They say they want peace with us. But I'll tell you how they want peace with us. They want us as laborers—without rights. They don't want to be on an equal basis with us, to live with us as two independent states. They think that by the power they have they can rule all of the Arab countries. The extremists think that way. They talk about the other part of Israel, which is Jordan. And what will come after Jordan? We don't know. The Israeli government must recognize our right to self-determination. But so long as it says, 'We won't recognize the PLO even if the PLO recognizes Israel,' what can we do?"

"The Israeli government argues," I returned, "that it's impossible to expect that Israel should recognize an organization that's bent on its destruction."

"But we say, 'How can we recognize someone who takes our land?'"

"Let's look at reality for a moment," I responded. "Israel has power here now. Israel has everything and the Palestinians have nothing."

"Yes! You are right!"

"And the Palestinians sometimes have friends and sometimes don't. Arab countries use them for their own needs."

"Yes! You are right!"

"And this is even the case with the Soviet Union. If it didn't serve their interests, they would drop the Palestinian cause."

"Yes!"

"In this situation, if I were a Palestinian, I would say to myself, 'I have nothing, the Israelis have everything. I want to do whatever I can to have something.'"

"So tell me what I can do."

"I think," I answered, "that there are a large number of people within Israel who would be willing, for the sake of security and peace, to allow the establishment of a Palestinian state. But they're frightened. They fear that given the feelings of the Palestinians, if they were given a Palestinian state they would move into it and then start talking about the liberation of the *rest* of Palestine. If you were an Israeli, you might also want to be reassured. You might ask, 'Why should I commit suicide?' "

"How can such an Israeli be reassured?"

"Maybe he can be reassured if people like you say, 'I agree there should be two countries here. And you should have the right to a country, and we should have the right to a country. I have no aspirations to take over Israel. And I define Israel as a country that exists within the borders before 1967, with some modifications in those borders that could be worked out. And also, because of the realities of geography, you would need a long period of time during which you would not be threatened militarily by armaments on the West Bank. And I'm willing to accept this, and to say right now that I'm willing to accept the right of Israel to exist within those borders; and all I ask is that we begin arranging for the establishment of a Palestinian state.' "

"Look," Natshe responded incredulously, "the Israelis have the power. So how can the Israelis be afraid? What we want is a comprehensive solution. We have to solve not only our problem here but also the problem of the Palestinians in other countries—in Syria, in Saudi Arabia. A Palestinian who has rights in Jaffa should either get compensation or be allowed to return. Take the Palestinian living in Damascus. You give him a choice. You say to him, 'Do you wish to live in Jaffa, in the Israeli state? Or do you wish to live in Hebron, in the Palestinian state?' He will choose. If he chooses to return to Jaffa, he will return, and accept the fact that he is going to Israel. If he wants to go to Hebron, or to any other place on the West Bank, then he will find a job, a home, and get compensation."

I asked Natshe why the Palestinians who live in Syria and other Arab countries didn't move to the West Bank when they could have—before 1967, when it was under Jordanian control.

"There were many problems," Natshe replied. "There were not enough jobs. This is a problem—that they didn't return," he admitted.

"Yes, it is a problem," I repeated. "Tell me something else. What about the problem in Haifa or in any of the places in Israel in which Palestinians lived before 1948? These cities now have almost totally Jewish populations. Realistically, it wouldn't work for Arabs to come back and claim a house or land in such a city."

"Look," Natshe said, "let's say an Arab has ten dunams in Israel. [One dunam equals a quarter of an acre.] And Israelis are now living on those ten dunams. Okay. For those ten dunams he should get compensation. And he should be able to live in Israel, like any other immigrant from Russia or America. And if he doesn't want to live in Israel, then he can take his money and live in the Palestinian state."

"You think there's room for a million Palestinian immigrants in the West Bank?"

"Yes, there's room."

"The official PLO position is that there should be a democratic state in Palestine which has Jews and Palestinians. Do you believe that such a thing would work?"

"Realistically, no. Because many Israelis want their own state."

"And the Palestinians?"

"Yes, many Palestinians want their own state too. But I think that if there are two states in the area and there is peace, then after some time—say, ten years or twenty years—the borders will not be a problem between them. They will be able to cross borders to work in each other's country."

"For many years," I said, "there has been a great deal of difficult and painful feeling on the part of Palestinians, especially those growing up outside Israel. Those who grew up in the camps grew up with powerful feelings of animosity against Israel."

"Yes, you are right."

"Only a dreamer would imagine that these feelings would disappear overnight. And even if the official position of the government of a newly established Palestinian state would be the acceptance of Israel and the rejection of any aspiration to reclaim the whole of Palestine, still, surely there would be some Palestinians who would resist this position, who would not be happy with it."

"Yes."

"Let's say," I went on, "that you were the president of the new Palestinian state, or someone else were—Yasser Arafat, say, or Abu Musa—"

"Yes—"

"And here are these people who are now saying, five years after the establishment of the Palestinian state, or ten years after, 'Now we have to liberate the rest of Palestine. We shed all this blood—' "

"Yes—"

" '—and now we have to liberate the rest of our homeland.' "

Natshe sighed. I went on. "Palestinians have been saying this for many years—for thirty years and more. This feeling can't just disappear overnight. Moreover, it's a popular feeling. It wouldn't be just 2 percent of the Palestinians who would feel it; it would probably be more. Who knows how many? Maybe 20 percent, 30 percent. I don't know how many it would be, but it would be, I think, many."

Natshe nodded agreement.

"Would you, as president of the Palestinian state, suppress these people?" I asked him. "Would you throw them into jail if they tried to cross the border into Israel?"

Natshe rejected my dark scenario, which was in fact a rendition of a common Israeli nightmare. "You are assuming something that doesn't exist. We have to think of what would happen in an actual state of peace. If you consider the Palestinian in a refugee camp, you have to understand that he is against the Israeli state and wants to kill any Israeli he meets because since 1948 he has been living in a miserable state as if in jail; he sees that his homeland has been taken away from him and hears everyone around him in the country in which he is living calling him a foreigner. But look at what has happened to the Arabs who have lived in the West Bank and in Gaza. Until

1967 they assumed that any Israeli who would meet them would kill them; and many of them also felt that if they met an Israeli they would kill *him*. But after 1967 things changed. Israelis and Arabs have begun to see and speak to each other. And now these Arabs know that there are some Israelis who are aware of our concerns and aspirations, and who agree that we should have our rights. So things have changed, and I don't necessarily view an Israeli as an enemy. I can distinguish between Israelis. I can say, This is a friend; this is Gush Emunim; this is Tehiya [the Renaissance Party, which favors annexation of the West Bank]; this is Peace Now. So let's say a Palestinian from, say, the El Yarmuk camp, in Damascus, who has been living in bad conditions as a foreigner in Syria, comes to the Palestinian state. He gets compensation for his lost property in Israel and has enough to live on here. He will have contact with Israelis—by working in Israel or by commerce with them—and he will change his point of view. Why do you assume that he will be an enemy of the Israelis?"

Because Natshe had returned several times to the theme of compensation for the property lost by Arabs who had left the part of Palestine that became Israel, I asked him about the argument, often made by Israelis, that at about the same time that Arabs were fleeing their homes and losing their property in Israel, Jews were fleeing their homes and losing their property in Arab countries—probably in equal or greater numbers, and probably with greater material losses. What about the argument that the losses balance each other out, and that compensation has therefore, in that sense, already taken place?

Natshe wouldn't accept this. Compensation is still very important, he said. Let Iraq and Egypt compensate the Jews who lost their property in those countries; and let Israel compensate the Palestinians who lost their property in Israel. He went on to tell me of the compensation that he and his family were expecting. "My uncle had an orchard near Tel Aviv, in a place which they call now Ramat Hasharon. It was 170 dunams. And we ourselves had three houses and land which we also lost in 1948. So it's obvious that compensation is necessary."

Finally I pointed out Natshe's window, in the direction in which I thought Kiryat Arba must lie. The settlements were growing up around him every day, I said. He could spend his days and years talking about the details of compensation, but meanwhile the settlements would continue to be built. Jews would continue to move into places that they considered to be their patrimony. And soon, I said, it would be a closed subject. It would be too late. The Jews would be back in the Land of Israel, and there would be no Palestinian state in the West Bank to talk about.

Paradoxically, Natshe relaxed. He smiled. All that talk about compensation, about recognition, about a democratic binational state, about boundaries and partition plans, suddenly appeared absurd and irrelevant. Natshe's eyes seemed to grow as old as the hills toward which my finger was pointing. He said there was time, plenty of time. "Now," he told me, "the Israelis have the power. And the Arabs don't have the power. But in ten years, in twenty years, in thirty years, who knows? At some time the Arabs will have the power, the forces will be on the side against Israel, *we* will have the power. And then we will see what will be."

6

The Jew Is a
Stranger in My House

The archaeological news out of the West Bank in October of 1983 was that an altar had been unearthed in the very spot the Bible says Joshua built his altar after leading the children of Israel into the promised land. It was the kind of news that doesn't gladden the hearts of West Bank Arabs. Nor is it the kind of news that West Bank Jewish settlers ignore. For them, it's continuing proof that they've returned to the Land of Israel.

The stone altar—a 27-by-21-foot structure near the peak of Mount Ebal—not only fits the description of an altar that Joshua built on that mountain but also is the kind of altar that, in Deuteronomy, God had instructed his people to build after crossing the Jordan. The archaeologists found sheep bones, ashes, and a dark substance on the altar that may have been blood from animal sacrifices; and based on carbon 14 testing, the site was dated to the twelfth century B.C., the time when the children of Israel probably did cross the Jordan.

The 3,100-foot Mount Ebal is located less than a mile north of the Arab town of Nablus, which is in turn a mile west of the archaeological mound that was the site of the biblical town of Shechem. Though Nablus is not in the same spot as Shechem, it is called in Hebrew by the ancient town's name.

Shechem itself—the ancient town, that is—figures prominently in Jewish history. It was to Shechem that Abraham came, and it was there that he built his own altar at Elon [the terebinth, or oak, of] Moreh. Jacob bought land there, and his sons Simeon and Levi destroyed the city after their sister Dina was raped. Joseph was buried in Shechem on land purchased by his father, Jacob. It was the place of the great covenant for which Joshua assembled the tribes of Israel. And it was at Shechem, years later, that the ten northern tribes repudiated Solomon's son and crowned Jeroboam in his place. In 107 B.C. Shechem, which by then had been taken from Jewish hands, was destroyed by John Hyrcanus, the nephew of the founder of Hanukah, Judah Maccabee, in the course of Hyrcanus' battles to reestablish the Jewish state after centuries of expulsions and foreign domination. Earth was spread over the city to bury it forever.

Almost two centuries later, in 72 A.D., Vespasian founded a city between Mounts Ebal and Gerizim, very near the site of Shechem. It is this city, which he called Flavia Neopolis, which came to be known as Nablus. Favored by abundant water, it prospered. The Arabs conquered it in 636; and though Jews lived in it, as well as Samaritans, it has been an overwhelmingly Arab Moslem town ever since. Estimates of the current population range from 60,000, a figure offered by Israelis, to 100,000, the figure most often cited by Arabs.

On June 7, 1979, a group of Gush Emunim settlers took over a piece of land near uninhabited land not far from Nablus and announced the establishment of Elon Moreh, named after the place in Shechem where Abraham had built his altar. A week later, seventeen Arab landowners, represented by an Arab lawyer and a Jewish one, sued for the return of the land, which had been theirs. The Israeli Supreme Court, in an unprecedented decision, ordered that the land be returned. Private land in an occupied territory, the court held, could be temporarily seized for military purposes under Section 52 of the Hague Convention, but this seizure had been made for a political, not a military, purpose, that of establishing a permanent, not a temporary, settlement. As a result of this judgment, it became clear that it would be possible to build Jewish settlements only on land that had been held by the Jordanian government prior to the 1967 war, that was without private title, or that had been purchased from individual Arabs.

Ordered to leave Elon Moreh, the settlers resisted. They argued that the Hague Convention didn't apply, since the West Bank was not "occupied" territory but, rather, "reoccupied"— reoccupied by Jews after years of exile. The Israeli government, however, acceded to the demand of the court and in February of 1980 removed the settlers to a new site on government land five miles away. After a postponement to allow for a circumcision at the settlement, flatbed trucks arrived to remove the trailers in which the settlers had been living. Some settlers lay down on the road to block them. One ran out of her trailer screaming, "You'll begin dismantling this settlement and you'll end up in Tel Aviv!" Another stood in front of his trailer chanting the Hebrew prayer traditionally said in times of impending martyrdom, "Hear O Israel!," and pulled up his shirtsleeve to reveal a tattooed number. "Look at that," he said. "I was in Auschwitz." His son, together with the leader of the settlement, led him away.

Following the court-ordered removal of Elon Moreh, Menachem Begin's government announced plans to build more settlements, and Begin himself later vowed that Israel would never leave the West Bank. Elon Moreh and Yamit, the city evacuated when Israel gave the Sinai back to Egypt in fulfillment of the Camp David accords, became for the Gush Emunim and their supporters geographical tragedies to be remembered and never repeated. For Israelis opposed to the settlements, however, they became harbingers of even more painful things to come.

It was against this background of history and violence that I visited Nablus to talk with Bassam Shaka'a, recently dismissed as mayor of the town by the Israeli authorities and himself a target of considerable violence.

On June 2, 1980, Shaka'a, while turning the ignition key of his car, set off a bomb that blew off his lower legs. On the same day, in the same way, another West Bank mayor, Karim Khalaf of Ramallah, lost a foot. And in El Bireh, also on the same day, Mayor Ibrahim Tawil was saved from a classic military "side-charge" that had been buried in a flower bed alongside his garage; the Israeli bomb-disposal expert who was sent to the scene, a Druse, accidentally touched the trip wire and was blinded.

As it happened, these attacks on the West Bank mayors were made on precisely the last day of the thirty-day mourning period for six Jewish settlers who had been shot outside Beit Hadassah, in Hebron. One resident of the Jewish West Bank settlement of Gush Etzion, appalled by the emergence of terrorism among Jewish settlers, told a *Jerusalem Post* reporter, "I have suddenly begun to realize that there are people out there who make Rabbi Moshe Levinger look moderate."

The West Bank mayors who were the targets of the June 1980 attacks were among the most radical on the West Bank, at least from the Israeli perspective: they actively supported the PLO, and according to some Israelis they organized their townspeople in every way they could to resist and obstruct the Israeli occupation, even to the point of terrorism and other forms of violence. Of this group of mayors, probably the most active and popular, and certainly the best known, was Bassam Shaka'a of Nablus.

The same Arab journalist who had accompanied me to the home of Mustafa Natshe accompanied me to the home of Bassam Shaka'a. The entrance to Shaka'a's house was guarded by Israeli soldiers, who checked my passport and then lingered over my friend's identity papers. Finally, after they had registered our names on a visitors' form, we were let through. Shaka'a, in a white cotton gown, was waiting for us on his porch. Though the gown was long, the stump of his right leg, amputated at the knee, was visible from time to time as he sat.

The mutilation of his legs, Shaka'a said, had had a powerful effect on his daughter, who had been four years old at the time. "She saw everything," Shaka'a explained. "She wasn't able to live in the house after that. She always wanted to live somewhere else. And when I came back from treatment after the bombing, she didn't accept me. She was always looking at my legs. It took many months before she was comfortable, before she was able to forget. She's all right now."

Shaka'a wanted to know if the Israeli guards had harassed me. They were always, he said, harassing him and his guests. "They have no shame at all. And they do it all under the orders of their superiors. I protest all these things, I go outside and curse them. I tell them, 'You are dirty!' And they take me to the military headquarters and carry out an investigation. I complain about the soldiers' behavior. But the soldiers deny that they harass me." And, Shaka'a added, the soldiers were always harassing those of his townspeople who wanted to talk with him: "They want to make people afraid. It's a kind of psychological warfare against me, and against the people who wanted to deal with me. They failed to kill me physically, and now they want to kill me socially. They want to cut off my relations with my people. Journalists for the *Jerusalem Post* and *Haaretz* have written that the Israeli military authorities simply want to kill me while I'm alive."

Shaka'a scoffed at my characterization of the Israeli occupation of the West Bank as benign. As far as he was concerned, it was deeply malignant. It was malignant, he said, to establish a Jewish school in the middle of his town, next to a grave traditionally considered to be Joseph's. It was malignant to increase taxes and the price of electricity. It was malignant to dismiss him from his position as mayor and deport those Arabs who resisted the Israeli occupation. And it was malignant to harass not only him and his Arab supporters but also those Israelis who visited him out of sympathy and solidarity.

Israelis, Shaka'a insisted, had nothing to fear—from the Palestinians, from the Arabs in general, or even from the Soviet Union. "They're very strong," he explained, "but they always make themselves appear to be victims. They always say they're victims, but they're criminals."

Shaka'a saw little hope for an accommodation with Israel. It was the Labor Party, he reminded me, not Begin's Likud, that had started the settlements. Negotiations with an occupier, he stressed, were impossible. And besides, how could any Arab negotiate with an Israel bent on ruthless expansion: "From the beginning, since before 1947, before the creation of the State of Israel, the Israelis had the intention of creating an Israel that stretched from the Nile to the Euphrates. The 1948 borders were simply the beginning. They were willing to start with them, with the aim of expanding the state."

For Shaka'a, as for Natshe, every Israeli action was part of a plan to take over more and more Arab land. "What the Israelis want to do," he stressed, "is to annex the land. They want the land but they don't want us. So they want to negotiate with the Jordanians so that the Jordanians will help them work against the Palestinian nation. And this is the entire philosophy behind the tactic of creating a civilian administration or working for 'autonomy.' And I can prove this. I said this to the Israeli military governor, Yossi Cohen, I said, 'Look, you want to annex the land. So annex us with the land!' And he said, 'We don't accept you as citizens.' "

I asked Shaka'a what he would say if the Israelis would be willing to grant the Palestinian Arabs full citizenship rights were they to annex the West Bank.

"I wouldn't accept it!" Shaka'a returned. "What would that do for the refugees?" He went on. "My brother-in-law, Salah Bustani, when he was speaking with the head of the Israeli civilian administration, asked him how come he didn't recognize the reality—that the city of Nablus is an Arab city, that the area is Arab. And the Israeli answered, 'Look, Salah, these are not the facts. If you want to know the true facts, search inside the ground.' And he went back two thousand years, when they had a state for three hundred years. And anything that happened after that, in their view, was just like dirty materials that went against their view of things. And we wouldn't be surprised if they simply took us with cars at some point and just threw us out."

As for the Jews, Shaka'a said, they had no right at all to be in the West Bank. "It's against international law! It's against the principle of human rights. They have no right to live here. If they want peace, they have to withdraw from here. I'm surprised when anybody thinks that they have such rights. You're an American. Could anybody build a state in your country?" Besides, Shaka'a asked me, "how can I accept those criminals? They cannot settle here." After suggesting that it was the Israeli authorities themselves, or people they knew, who had planted the bomb in his car, he added, "I cannot accept them on my land! I wouldn't respect anyone who *would* accept them!"

Regarding the right of the Jews to stay in the part of Palestine that became Israel, Shaka'a was willing to say only that that was a matter for negotiation once there was a Palestinian state and arrangements had been made to resettle or compensate the Arab refugees. When I suggested that Israel would be unlikely ever to accept a Palestinian state unless Arabs had already accepted Israel's right to exist, Shaka'a insisted that I was wrong. Eventually, he predicted, Israel would bow to pressure, both internal and external. Eventually Israel would be forced in one way or another to accept a Palestinian state in the West Bank. And toward that end there could be no compromise. The only position a West Bank Arab could take was the position of the PLO. He himself could never accept the occupation. "What would they say if I accepted this occupation? They would say I was a quisling! Or a Pétain. What would happen to the quisling Bassam Shaka'a?"

Shaka'a repeatedly volunteered that he didn't hate the Israelis, despite what they had done to him. Yet the outrage that he expressed toward Israel was so powerful and so deep that I had difficulty distinguishing it from hatred. He saw himself and his people reduced to vassals, or worse, and hurled back eons to a brutal and lawless time. "In what stage of civilization are we living?" he asked, growing red with indignation. "Do we live in a forest? Are we beasts? Am I meat to be eaten by the beasts? For the Israelis I am not a human! I am not a he and not a she!"

An Israel that could reduce him to such a state, Shaka'a made clear, was not an Israel that he could ever accept—and certainly not one that he could ever consider a friend of his people. "Can I consider you a friend," he asked, "if you want my house?"

The question startled me. Shaka'a had chosen precisely the same metaphor that Moshe Levinger, some days before, had chosen in trying to explain to me, with wild eyes, how impossible it seemed to him to compromise on the question of Israeli sovereignty over the West Bank. The Arab, Levinger had said, was a stranger in his house, had taken it over, and now wanted it, or part of it, for himself. If a stranger had taken over *my* house, would *I* give him part of it? So how could I expect the Jews to give up part of *their* house to the Arabs?

And now the Moshe Levinger of the West Bank Arabs, Bassam Shaka'a, was using the same metaphor, and drawing me into it. Yet in Shaka'a's version it was the Jew who was the stranger and the Arab whose home had been invaded. "How can I consider you a friend," he asked again, as the sun dropped behind the Samarian Hills overlooking his town, "when I know that you want my house?" And though he was speaking rhetorically, and the "you" in question was not the I sitting before him, I nevertheless turned, as if to avoid his gaze.

In the Land of *Al-Fajr*

Before I visited the West Bank, Amos Oz, a well-known Israeli novelist, spent some time there as well. His interviews with West Bankers, both Jews and Arabs, as well as his interviews with Jews in Israel were published to applause and outrage as articles in the Israeli Labor Party newspaper *Davar*. Those articles subsequently became chapters in a book published in Israel and then, a year later, in the United States, under the title *In the Land of Israel*.

Among the Arabs whom Oz interviewed were three editors at *Al-Fajr*, a Palestinian newspaper published in East Jerusalem; the full name of the newspaper is *Al-Fajr Al-Arabi*, or "The Arab Dawn." The publisher, a Palestinian named Paul Ajlouny, spends much of his time in the United States. He is said to be wealthy but by most accounts is himself not the source of the newspaper's money; that source, Israelis insist and some Palestinians agree, is the PLO. While the major East Jerusalem daily *Al-Quds*—which has a circulation of 10,000 to 15,000 and is financially supported by Jordan—reflects conservative West Bank views and favors Jordanian policies, *Al-Fajr*, with a circulation of 3,000 to 5,000, is more nationalistic and pro-PLO, considers *Al-Quds* reactionary to the point of being traitorous, and has even urged a boycott of it.

Like other Arab newspapers in East Jerusalem, *Al-Fajr* is

heavily censored by the Israeli government. While the Israeli press is subject to censorship on military and security grounds, the Arab press in those areas is censored also on political ones. Articles that support the PLO position, that question the right of Israel to exist, that advocate the destruction or elimination of Israel, or that could, in the judgment of the censor, inflame Palestinian nationalism or incite Arabs to violence, are routinely disallowed. *Al-Fajr* informs its readers of the number of articles it submitted to the censor that were not permitted publication or that were partially censored.

Nevertheless, the newspaper manages to be consistently and sharply critical of Israeli policies. It devotes much of its space and energy to reports of Israeli maltreatment of Arab West Bank residents, and ingeniously succeeds in skirting much of the censorship by reprinting articles from the Israeli press that are critical of the government. And, despite the censorship, Arab journalists have admitted that *Al-Fajr* is not only far freer than any West Bank newspaper was before 1967, during the Jordanian occupation, but also freer than almost all newspapers in the Arab world, including the Palestinian newspapers in Jordan.

According to Oz, the *Al-Fajr* editors he interviewed recognized that Israel existed and had to continue to exist. At least two of them, and probably all three, seemed willing to distance themselves from the PLO and to accept the State of Israel and its people without hesitation. They were open, realistic, accommodating, and sympathetic—precisely the kinds of Palestinians who would have to exist for the programs of the Israeli peace movement, particularly Peace Now, to make sense. Oz is in fact a prominent spokesman for Peace Now.

The *Al-Fajr* editors, for their part, found themselves, after the publication of Oz's articles, in deep trouble. Palestinians in the West Bank and elsewhere attacked them for being so accommodating and for undermining the appearance of West Bank Arab unity in support of the official PLO position. The editors responded by denying the accuracy of Oz's reports on their conversations; they hadn't said, they said, what Oz had said they had said. Oz had, in short, engaged in wishful report-age; he had, they insisted, made it, or part of it, up.

Oz's only response to this and other accusations of distor-tion and inaccuracy—leveled at him not only by West Bank Arabs but even more energetically by Israelis he interviewed—was a cryptic comment at the end of a list of criticisms he appended to his book: "So be it."

At the time of my own visit to the West Bank, Oz's articles and book had already appeared, and I was aware of the contro-versy they had provoked and of the ill effects they had had on the *Al-Fajr* editors who had agreed to talk to him. I wondered whether any *Al-Fajr* editors would be willing, after that, to talk to me. I decided, though, that it was worth a try.

Oz had talked to editors of the Arabic edition of the news-paper. I went instead to the offices of the English edition of the newspaper, the *Al-Fajr Jerusalem Palestinian Weekly,* which are located in a small, one-story building on a quiet residential street in East Jerusalem a few blocks from the Old City's walls.

The offices themselves were a beehive of journalistic activ-ity. Though shabby—hardly the picture I had envisioned of PLO-channeled-Gulf-oil-money-luxuriousness—they were full of enthusiasm and energy, much of it provided by young Americans sympathetic to the Palestinian Arab cause. A pair of Norwegian journalists, also sympathetic to the Palestinian cause, were paying their respects, their stark blondness con-trasting sharply with the dark features of the Palestinians around them.

Sam'an Khoury, then the weekly's managing editor, said he would be happy to talk to me. He invited me into his utilitarian office, decorated, as were the other offices in the building, with posters portraying the repressed spirit of the Palestinian people. Above his head, for example, was a drawing of a gaunt figure being rudely bound and muzzled.

A trim, athletic man of thirty-five with short hair and a mustache, Khoury was dressed in a black pullover shirt and jeans. His English, learned at a Christian missionary school, was flowing and precise. He told me that he had been born in

Bethlehem in June 1948, three weeks after his parents had fled
Jerusalem as a result of the Arab–Israeli fighting. Three months
later they returned; and he has lived in the city ever since, with
the exception of two years, 1977–1979, spent in an Israeli prison for membership in the Democratic Front for the Liberation
of Palestine. While in prison Khoury learned, he said, "how to
be patient, how to read thoroughly, and how to live socially
with fifty other people in the room."

I don't know whether Oz would have been successful in
getting Khoury to voice an opinion different from the PLO's, or
whether he would have portrayed Khoury as accommodating
no matter what Khoury would have told him. For my part, I
couldn't budge him from the PLO line of nonrecognition of
Israel, despite extended, almost desperate attempts to do so:

REICH: If you were to have to guess about the percentage of the
Palestinian people who would be willing to give up their
hope of returning to the part of Palestine that is now Israel
in exchange for the establishment of a Palestinian state on
the West Bank, what percentage would you guess that
would be?

KHOURY: The majority. Why do you think the support for the
resolutions of the Palestinian National Council is so strong
now? Why wasn't it there in 1965 and 1967? Why wasn't it
there in the occupied territories [the West Bank and Gaza]
even in 1973? It's because these same people who have been
living under occupation understand the realities.

REICH: And you believe that if they had their own state they
would give up any claim of national ownership of what is
now the State of Israel.

KHOURY: As a prediction, I would say that the possibilities of
agreeing to this argument are much greater than the refusal.
The refusal can never prevail. There might be a minority
who would be against this, but they would not prevail.

REICH: And into which camp would you fall?

KHOURY: I would fall into the camp of wanting to live in this state independently and freely and of not bothering others and of them not bothering me.

REICH: And the others would include the State of Israel, which you would recognize.

KHOURY: This might include a State of Israel which would be recognized through negotiations.

REICH: And you would favor that yourself.

KHOURY: I would respect the outcome of these negotiations.

REICH: But you're also a human being. You have human thoughts, human feelings. You must have an opinion on this as well. You must have a view about this. If you were sitting in a meeting, people would be arguing about this. Which side would you take?

KHOURY: If I was a representative, then I would represent the Palestinians' view.

REICH: But if you were an ordinary Palestinian—

KHOURY: If I was not a representative, then I would adhere to the position of the representative.

REICH: [Exasperated] But the representative is representing you!

KHOURY: I don't feel the ability, under occupation, to say my point of view.

REICH: But why not?

KHOURY: This is part of living under occupation.

REICH: It seems to me, if you want my honest opinion, that you're hiding behind a position. You're not allowing yourself free expression. This is a crucial question—*the* crucial question. It's vital to the future of the Palestinian people. The Palestinian people are going to have to make these decisions; many have made them personally, in their own minds, and you've acknowledged that. So I'm asking you what decision you've made in your own mind. And you're answering like a politician. You're evading the question.

KHOURY: I cannot say that I can say freely whether I recognize the State of Israel or not because I am living under occupation. And even if I was living in Syria, I don't think I can say it.

REICH: [More exasperated] But that's a political statement. You're an intelligent man. You've developed many opinions. And this is one of the crucial issues. It's something about which you've surely developed some ideas. And you're telling me that you're under occupation, that you're sitting in jail; and I understand your position that, as an organized people, the Palestinians refuse to make a statement on this point. But it's not as if you can't think. It's not as if someone has electrocuted your mind. Surely you have a view on this as an individual.

KHOURY: [By now also exasperated] Even what I am going to say is influenced by the environment in which I live, which is the occupation. I'm telling you that I cannot be truthful about what I am saying.

REICH: All right, this is a peculiar argument, but I'll accept it for a moment. You're saying—it doesn't seem to me to be a human argument, human beings don't quite behave this way—you're saying that you can't think clearly under these circumstances.

KHOURY: No, I'm saying that I can't express myself as freely as I would want to express myself.

REICH: So who's stopping you?

KHOURY: The occupation!

REICH: But there's nobody here. No police, no guns. Who's stopping you?

KHOURY: It's a product of living for sixteen years under the occupation!

REICH: You mean the day after there is a state established you're going to be able to suddenly think freely, that before that you couldn't?

KHOURY: I can express myself freely under those circumstances.

REICH: You mean there's something you know but you can't say because you're afraid to say it?

KHOURY: No. Whatever I say is going to be influenced by the mere existence of me under the occupation. And not only the occupation, but the whole environment around me. During the Jordanian occupation I felt as a Palestinian, but

I couldn't say it. Now I feel as a Palestinian, and I can say it. And maybe as a Palestinian now I say that the reality says that if we want to live in peace and freely, there should be two states in Palestine. But I even suspect that *this* may be the product of living for sixteen years under occupation. I don't know whether it's that or whether it is a reality. I don't know whether it's a product of the environment or whether it's a clear way of thinking on my part.

REICH: Let me restate this and ask you if what I understand you to be saying is correct. You're saying, "I cannot even answer you honestly because I don't know how I would answer you if I were truly free. If I were truly free and in my own state my feelings might be different from the way they are now. Right now the reality that I see is that the Palestinians have nothing and the Israelis have everything. Of course"—I'm putting words in your mouth, I know—"if I were to say something now, maybe I would say that I accept Israel as a state only because it's all around me and I'm occupied by this powerful force, a force that won all these wars. For much of my life under Israeli occupation—I even lived for two years in an Israeli jail—Israel has been a powerful reality around me. Therefore, of course I have to say that Israel is powerful, it's a powerful reality around me, and I have to accept it. But if I were living in my own state I might think differently. I would have a different perspective. I would feel liberated. Maybe I wouldn't feel the pressure of this other state. And maybe I would be able to see things differently"—and here I may be injecting my own interpretation of what you said—"and maybe I would feel so free that I would be able to say that maybe Israel *doesn't* have the right to exist here."

KHOURY: No. What I'm stating exactly is that the situation that every Palestinian in the world, not only under Israeli occupation, is in, in one way or another influences that Palestinian's opinion. And the only way that this opinion can be actually representative of the Palestinian people is when this Palestinian people and its individuals are actually free.

Khoury and I tortured each other like this for several rounds. An engaging man, possessed of patience, grace, warmth, and generosity, he deserved better from me. And perhaps I, in my intense wish to make him take a personal position, a human position, for his own sake and for what I thought was the sake of his people, deserved better from him. Still, I felt that the issues we were discussing were in fact among the central ones, ones that would have to be solved, or disposed of, if any solution were to be achieved; and I felt I had to raise them, even if doing so brought us both to verbal grief.

The one matter I raised that disturbed Khoury—indeed, that shook him—had to do with the disunity of the PLO itself. The split in the organization between Abu Musa's Syrian-backed faction and Yasser Arafat's loyalists, I observed, had weakened it so much that it was unlikely to be able to mount effective diplomatic or military efforts for a long time. Given the steady spread and growth of Jewish settlements in the West Bank, I asked, wasn't it time for the West Bank Palestinians to take matters into their own hands and offer to negotiate with the Israelis before there was nothing left to negotiate about?

Though clearly agitated about the PLO split, Khoury refused to accept my suggestion. He continued to insist on the importance of backing the PLO and of not taking independent initiatives. He admitted that the split did indeed worry him, and that at times it had worried him enough to make him consider the very option I had just raised. But he concluded that the split was temporary, and that unity behind the PLO was still the only position a West Bank Palestinian could take. He insisted that the PLO was all the Palestinians had, and that there were no other forces they could rely on, whether Syrian or Jordanian. No Arab regime, he observed with disgust, had ever had the Palestinians' interests at heart, including Hussein's.

Our meeting ended in amity, despite the repeated pleas on my part that he be realistic, and despite the repeated insistence on his that I had to understand that the PLO's way was the only way. I told Khoury that I had a next-door neighbor in Washington, a surgeon, whose father, a revered Palestinian poet named Abu Salma, had recently died; and that I'd heard that *Al-Fajr* had published a memorial to him. Khoury remembered it; the memorial issue had, on its front page, a photo of the poet being embraced by Yasser Arafat. He found it in his files and carefully copied the issue for me so that I could take it, together with his regards, to the beloved poet's son.

8

Israel Is a Strange Body in the Middle East

More than once, Palestinian Arabs who have strayed from the PLO line, or who have in some other way undercut the PLO's agenda or embarrassed its program, have been punished for their deviations. Some have been chastised. Others have been assassinated.

It is for this reason that I will not identify the Palestinian with whom I spent the most time while visiting the West Bank. He ultimately talked to me in ways in which other politicized Palestinians did not allow themselves to talk. For that I was grateful; and for that I'll call him only Karim.

I met Karim in the offices of a pro-PLO Palestinian organization. I had come there to interview its director and had found Karim instead. He was the only one working that Sunday, and we began to talk.

At first Karim educated me about the development of Palestinian nationalism since the 1967 war. He analyzed the relationships between the Palestinians and the various Arab countries, mostly to demonstrate how perfidious those countries have been with regard to Palestinian aspirations. The only people the Palestinians can trust, he concluded, are themselves, and it's for that reason that they have taken a united stand behind the PLO.

The PLO's positions, Karim pointed out, have changed over

the years. "After 1967, the PLO raised the slogan of a secular democratic state in all of Palestine in which all Jews and Moslems and Christians would have the right to stay. Whether the Jews who came after 1948 would stay was a debatable issue. There would be no State of Israel. After 1974 this slogan was changed. They decided that there should be a Palestinian state in the West Bank. The rejectionists refused this slogan, wanting to liberate all of Palestine. Eventually, all of the PLO factions agreed on this slogan without recognizing Israel. So the rejectionists want to establish a Palestinian state in the West Bank and not recognize Israel, so as to keep open the option of liberating the rest of Palestine. The others want to establish a Palestinian state on the West Bank and then solve the refugee problem by having them either return to their original homes in Israel or get compensation." It was a mistake, Karim went on, for the Arabs not to accept the UN partition plan of 1947. "It would have been better for us. Now we are much better in diplomacy."

I tried at every opportunity to pry Karim loose from his undeviating allegiance to the official PLO positions. Surely, I suggested, he had his own views. Surely there was no single truth, as the split in the PLO itself demonstrated. Surely even the PLO might not be infallible; it's at least possible that another approach, another position, might work better. Surely he understood that an organization like the PLO tends to regard any attempt at compromise as betrayal, which makes it difficult, if not impossible, to take advantage of opportunities for accommodation that may arise. I complained that with his unquestioning acceptance of PLO slogans he sounded a little like a Soviet official. Except that, I added, even Soviet officials sometimes speak frankly when they're speaking in private. Couldn't he?

At first he said he couldn't. The PLO was the only good thing that had ever happened to his people; if it had weaknesses and disadvantages, and even splits, they were less important than its strengths.

But the more we talked, the more times we visited, the more

we traveled through his homeland, the more questions I asked
him about his life and views and the more he asked me about
mine, the more he admitted to doubts.

He had doubts, first of all, about the wisdom of refusing to
offer Israel recognition in exchange for a Palestinian state—
recognition now, while there was still something in the West
Bank to make into a state. He too saw the hills slipping away,
saw the bulldozers and the settlements; and he too had begun
to wonder whether some way other than the PLO's might better enable the Palestinians to save what was left to be saved.

But he had other doubts, too. He wondered whether he or
the PLO or the Palestinians as a whole really could in their
hearts *ever* compromise—ever accept Israel in *any* form. "This
area," he explained, almost pleadingly, "is Arab. We have been
here for centuries. Israel's presence is strange here. It's a strange
body in the Arab homeland." And again: "The Palestinian people don't recognize Israel. It's a strange body in the Middle
East. The Palestinian people who were expelled from their land
want to return to their country."

Karim was talking not about the West Bank but about all of
western Palestine—including Israel. In his heart, he was saying,
Israel didn't belong there and shouldn't stay there; and that, he
added, was what was in the hearts of his fellow Palestinians, as
well. Didn't I agree? Did *I* really think that Israel had a place in
the Middle East?

Karim estimated that if it came to some kind of vote, 70
percent of the West Bank Palestinians would be willing to say
that they would recognize Israel once a Palestinian state was
established in the West Bank; he would, too. But what they
would say *after* the Palestinian state was established was, he
suspected, another story. The recognition of Israel by the Palestinians, he said, could never be anything other than a tactic—
because Israel was something that the Palestinians could never
really accept. What the dismissed mayor of Hebron, Mustafa
Natshe, had told me, Karim observed, was just a tactic. I had
told Karim that Natshe had said that, if Israel allowed the creation of a Palestinian state on the West Bank and offered any

Palestinian who had left during the 1948–1949 fighting the right to either return to his original home and property or obtain compensation for it, then some kind of peace, including some kind of recognition of some kind of Israel, was possible.

"That's just a tactic," Karim insisted. "And if the PLO ever brings itself to say that, it will also be a tactic. And I say that as someone who stands with the PLO. It's a tactic. There is no other way for someone to talk who has no power," Karim insisted. "We promise we will recognize Israel, but who knows what will happen in five years or ten years? What does it cost us to make such promises? If we gain through them a Palestinian state, then such promises are a good tactic. And if the balance of power changes in ten years—if Israel weakens internally, if America stops defending it, if the Arabs back us with their power—then things will change. The Palestinians will then be in a position to regain their rights in all of Palestine—to regain the rest of their homeland. I see no other way. We have to take what we can get now and see about the rest later. I see no peace coming—no real trust. Each side wants all of what the other side has. If there were only two people, one Arab and one Jew, it would be the same. There would be war. And it will always be that way. Always."

In saying that, Karim knew that he had admitted something dangerous—even something that his fellow Palestinians could call treacherous. After all, what he predicted the Palestinians would say after the creation of a Palestinian state was precisely what many Israelis, including many in the government, were predicting the Palestinians would say; and it was on the basis of that prediction that those Israelis had vowed never to give up the West Bank. So for a Palestinian to agree that those Israelis were right was indeed dangerous.

And it was because it was dangerous that I told Karim I would not identify him. Curiously, he said he didn't care. The whole matter saddened him, drained him. It was as if the tragedy had already happened; there was no hope, and therefore could be no fear.

One Gains Possession
of the Land of Israel
Only Through Suffering

On April 27, 1984, Israeli security forces dismantled bombs that had been placed on five Arab buses serving East Jerusalem and the West Bank. Within a few days, more than two dozen Jewish settlers from the West Bank and the Golan Heights, including Rabbi Moshe Levinger, were arrested, and many more were questioned. Israel's General Security Services, better-known as the Shin Bet, had, it turned out, infiltrated the settler underground.

On May 23, Israeli authorities filed criminal charges in Jerusalem District Court against twenty-five of the arrested settlers; those charges included murder, attempted murder, possession of weapons and explosives stolen from the Israeli army, and membership in a terrorist organization. Fifteen of the settlers were accused of having been involved, in a direct or indirect way, with the attempt to assassinate three West Bank Arab mayors in 1980, which left two of the mayors, including Bassam Shaka'a of Nablus, maimed, and an Israeli bomb-disposal expert blinded; four were accused of actually having planted the bombs used in that incident. In addition, six of the settlers were accused of having attacked the Islamic University in Hebron in the summer of 1983 with grenades and small-arms fire, leaving three Arabs killed and thirty-three wounded. Twelve of the twenty-five were charged with involvement in the thwarted bombings of the five Arab buses. And several were charged with other crimes, including seventeen in a conspiracy to blow up the Dome of the Rock, a Moslem holy place built on the spot once occupied by the First and Second Jewish Temples in Jerusalem; the planting of hand grenades next to a Moslem mosque in Hebron in December of 1983, which injured two Arabs; and the planting of two grenades in a Hebron soccer field in October of 1982, which also injured two Arabs.

On the day after the indictments of the settlers were filed, two Israeli army officers were also indicted for involvement in the bombings of the mayors, one for having provided information to the settlers that helped them place the bombs and one for having known the location of one of the bombs but having stood by and failed to warn the Israeli bomb-disposal expert in whose face that bomb exploded. Rabbi Levinger, who was held for more than a week, and who reportedly responded to his interrogators by lecturing and chastising them, was released without being charged. Another rabbi, the head of a yeshiva in Kiryat Arba who was running for a seat in the Knesset on the list of the Tehiya Party, was, however, arrested as part of the ongoing investigation. Upon his release, Levinger blamed the Israeli government for the violence; the government, he said, had done too little to protect the settlers from Arab attacks, forcing them to protect themselves.

Two days before the first indictments were handed down, Yitzhak Shamir, the Israeli prime minister, denounced the arrested settlers, many of whom had by then confessed to their acts, and several of whom had re-enacted them in the process of interrogation and confession. The accused settlers, Shamir told the Knesset, had damaged Israel's interests and the movement to build settlements in the West Bank. He took pains to distinguish between those settlers who had been involved in the attacks and the rest of the West Bank settler population. "It has become clear," he explained, "that this is a small group of people who were tempted into taking this crooked path. The decisive majority of the settlers of Judea and Samaria, the Golan Heights and the Gaza sector dissociate themselves from these acts without reservation. There is no justification for sullying the entire settlement enterprise with the crime of individuals who went astray."

Some of those individuals, however, were at the core of the settlement enterprise; in fact, according to Israel Harel, the secretary general of the Council of Jewish Settlements in Judea and Samaria, those who were charged with the bombings of the mayors were "the founding fathers" of the West Bank settlement movement. They were, he said, "not the thinkers, but the pioneers, the activists." And the bombings themselves, he stressed, were aimed at those who, it was believed, had given orders for an attack on a crowd of Jewish worshipers in Hebron that left six dead.

For his part, Shamir failed to distinguish between the settlers who were charged with bombing the mayors and those charged with random acts of violence: "It is worrisome and regrettable that after thirty-six years of independence there are still those among us who deny the authority of the state and who do not accept the fundamental principle that the Israeli government, and it alone, is responsible for Israel's security." Shamir added: "Our sages said, 'One gains possession of the Land of Israel only through suffering.' The existence of a Jewish group capable of committing such actions is part of this suffering."

Oddly enough, it was precisely this saying, drawn from the Talmud, that some of the arrested settlers themselves quoted after the arrests—except that, for them, what constituted the suffering, the *yisurim,* was not the existence of a Jewish terrorist group that had to be punished, but the punishment itself, which they saw as something they might have to bear as part of their struggle to gain possession of the Land of Israel.

In their view, it was the West Bank policies of the Israeli government, particularly during the late 1970s and early 1980s, that had made their actions necessary. In those years, they said, the Ministry of Defense, which had ultimate responsibility for the administration of the area, believed it could purchase the good will of the West Bank Arabs by maintaining restraint in its response to Arab violence. This led, in their judgment, to an increase in such violence on the part of Arabs, who assumed they would not be punished.

The best-known incidents of Arab violence were the most spectacular ones—incidents such as the 1980 killings of the six Jewish worshipers in Hebron. Between 1978 and February of 1984, four Israeli soldiers were killed and thirty-eight wounded in such "hostile terrorist activities," while sixteen Israeli civilians were killed and 115 wounded.

But it was the less-known and less-spectacular incidents—especially rock-throwing—that in some ways most disturbed the settlers; for it was these actions that, while less lethal, were more frequent, and made everyday life for the settlers precisely what they didn't want it to be: abnormal.

Rock-throwing was categorized by Israeli authorities under the heading of "public disturbances." Between April of 1982 and March of 1983, two Israelis were killed during public disturbances, and 174 were injured. According to some settlers, the frequency of injuries during such disturbances, particularly from rock-throwing, had been much higher several years before that, when Ezer Weizman, whom they considered to have been the most lenient of the defense ministers, was responsible for West Bank security.

The problem with rock-throwing, they maintained, was that settlers grew afraid to drive on West Bank roads or even walk outside their own settlements. Buses serving the settlements were regularly stoned, and settlers, children as well as adults, were often injured. The stonings took place even when Israeli soldiers patrolled the roads or sat in the buses.

The result, according to the settlers, was not only their fear of injuries to themselves and their families, but their sense that they couldn't live normal lives there—and, worse, the concern that other Jews, Israeli as well as foreign, were becoming reluctant to join them. For them, the rock-throwing had become a threat to the future of the settlement effort itself.

Often, the arrested settlers reported, they would meet with Israeli military authorities, hoping to put a stop to the problem.

Sometimes they suggested that the authorities restore some of
the measures that they said had been routine when Shimon
Peres had been responsible for the administration of the West
Bank; under Peres, who was minister of defense in the Labor
government that preceded the Likud's 1977 electoral victory,
the Israeli military authorities would exact heavy fines from the
fathers of the young Arabs throwing stones, and would sometimes deport them to Jordan. It was such measures that Ezer
Weizman, who later served as minister of defense under Menachem Begin, spurned as too harsh; and it was just such measures, the settlers insisted, that could stop the stonings.
Repeatedly, however, the lower-level Israeli authorities told the
complaining settlers that their hands were tied by orders direct-
ing them not to antagonize the local Arab population.

The rock-throwing, as well as the more lethal Arab terrorism, was, according to some settlers, ordered by the PLO itself
through its proxies in the West Bank. And chief among those
proxies, they contend, was the Palestine National Guidance
Committee, made up of several West Bank mayors and activists. It was the members of that committee, they believe, who
not only gave the orders to Arabs to stone Israeli cars, but also
to attack Jews with weapons—including the six Jews who were
killed in Hebron in May of 1980.

According to the charges filed by Israeli authorities against
the arrested settlers, some of them decided, soon after the Hebron attack, to respond with violence. And they chose as their
targets three of the members of the Palestine National Guidance Committee—Mayor Bassam Shaka'a of Nablus, Mayor
Karim Khalaf of Ramallah, and Mayor Ibrahim Tawil of El-
Bireh. As a result of the bombs these settlers placed, two of the
mayors—Shaka'a and Khalaf—were maimed. After those attacks, the settlers have said, the incidents of violence of all sorts
against Jews in the West Bank—shootings as well as rock-
throwing—decreased markedly.

The more random acts of anti-Arab violence that followed
the bombings of the mayors were often carried out in retaliation for random acts against Jews. A number of the arrested

settlers involved in the bombings of the mayors were said to have known nothing of the other acts; several reportedly deplored them as unjustified. Those settlers who were involved in the random acts, however, as well as their supporters, felt they were necessary as a means of showing the Arab population that if they condoned or abetted the random killing of Jews they would see random violence against their own people as well.

Some of the indicted settlers appeared surprised by their arrests. They considered themselves to be the successors of the Irgun and other underground Jewish organizations that had been created during the Palestine Mandate: just as Jews were unprotected by Britain in Palestine during the 1940s, they reasoned, so were they unprotected by Israel in the West Bank during the 1970s and 1980s. One defendant, said to be the head of a religious elementary school in Hebron, sent the following statement out of his cell a month after his arrest:

> Pure Jews, whose lives are dedicated to Zionist achievement, have been arrested for performing deeds for the sake of the security of the State of Israel and its citizens.
>
> They have been accused as if they were terrorists, as if they were an undergound against the state, which is more dear to them than anything!
>
> We must protest against this distortion and convince the authorities to consider these acts—which actually, due to the helplessness of the regime and its weakness before pressures from home and abroad, were illegal— according to their true motivation: on behalf of the state, on behalf of the people!
>
> "Should the righteous be as the wicked, may it be far from Thee" (Genesis 18:25).

The statement was signed, "Prisoners of Zion."

The arrests of the settlers and their indictments as terrorists immediately threw the settlement movement and its supporters, both in Israel and abroad, into crisis. While some protested the arrests, others protested the Jewish violence. When, for exam-

ple, Rabbi Levinger's twenty-four-year-old son Ephraim stood
vigil outside Prime Minister Shamir's residence, another Jew, an
American immigrant who had studied at the Mercaz Harav
Yeshiva, which was the source of much of the Gush Emunim
ideology, held a sign saying, "Whenever there is a desecration
of God's name, there is no honor for the rabbi." At the same
time, the Hesder Yeshiva movement, which supported the settlements with particular energy, and which had established a
number of religious schools in the West Bank, Gaza, and the
Golan Heights, set up a council, which it called Moriah, to
consider the Jewish violence, which it saw as a perversion of
its beliefs.

Other orthodox Jewish leaders in the settlements responded
similarly. The head of the Shevut Yisrael Yeshiva in Efrat, Rabbi Yehoshua Ben-Meir, condemned those who had been arrested as well as their crimes: "It's not that these people took the
law into their own hands. It's that they have taken government
into their hands." And, at a meeting between the leaders of the
Mercaz Harav Yeshiva in Jerusalem—which had been headed
by Rabbi Zvi Yehuda Kook, the spiritual father of the Gush
Emunim—and the leaders of the Gush Emunim itself, one grad-
uate of the yeshiva, who lives in the West Bank settlement of
Ofra, went so far as to accuse those arrested for the terrorist
crimes of being guilty of Sabbateanism—the seventeenth-cen-
tury movement begun by Sabbatai Zvi, who declared himself
the Messiah, who was believed and followed by many Jews,
and who eventually converted to Islam to escape death; the
settlers who had committed violent acts against Arabs, the Ofra
resident implied, had become false messiahs, perverting the
Jewish religion and leading their followers to the edge of destruction. Of the violent plans made by the underground settler
group, the one that provoked some of the greatest distress was
the one not carried out—the plan to destroy the mosques on
the Temple Mount. "That," Rabbi Ben-Meir said, "is plain
madness. It would have brought a war on all of Israel out of the
simplistic and false belief that that is what God wanted."

Perhaps the most visible rift among the West Bank settlers

themselves took place between those in the Etzion Bloc—some of them descendants of Jews who had been massacred there by Arabs in 1948—and the Gush Emunim, with the former group discussing the possibility of seceding from the Council of Settlements of Judea and Samaria. And outside the settlement movement, the arrests provoked considerable debate among Israelis. According to one poll, 80 percent of the Israeli population rejected the idea of settler violence. And, after Yuval Ne'eman, the Israeli Minister of Science and Development and a strong proponent of the settlements, was reported to have called the attack on the mayors "positive," he was rebuked by a spokesman for Prime Minister Shamir; by the energy minister, Yitzhak Modai, who responded, "Thou shalt not murder, even for political ends"; by former President Yitzhak Navon; by former Defense Minister Ezer Weizman; by members of the settlement of Alon Shvut, who called Ne'eman's remarks "disgusting"; and by twenty-one of Israel's leading intellectuals—including the president of the Israel Academy of Science, the president of the Weizmann Institute, and the president of the Hebrew University, who issued a statement condemning him.

But of the rifts provoked by the news that a violent underground movement existed among the settlers, perhaps the most painful one of all was formed within the hearts of individual settlers themselves—the rift between loyalty to the ideal of settling the Land of Israel and loyalty to the leaders of the settlement movement itself, of whom some were now charged with actions that most of the settlers found abhorrent.

"Should we in Gush Emunim go through a profound process of soul-searching, a *heshbon nefesh*?" one settler asked rhetorically when interviewed by an Israeli journalist for the *Jerusalem Post*, Yosef Goell. The settler, Shifra Blass, of Ofra, was a spokesperson for the eighty settlements that belonged to the Yesha Council—the acronym for the Hebrew words Yehuda (Judea), Shomron (Samaria), and Aza (Gaza); I had myself interviewed her in her home some months before the arrests. Having been born in La Crosse, Wisconsin, having grown up in Chambersburg, Pennsylvania, where her father was the only orthodox Jew, and having graduated from Barnard College in New York City, Blass emigrated to Israel in the early 1970s. When I had spoken with her, she had seemed firm in her conviction that the Jews had a greater right to Judea and Samaria than did the Arabs, but also firm in her feelings that the Jews had to do everything possible to accord Arabs full civil rights in the area. Faced with the Israeli reporter's questions on the day Rabbi Levinger's arrest was made known, she seemed just as firm about those convictions and feelings, but shaky, even confused, about the leadership of the settlement movement. "I'm still overwhelmed by the news about Rabbi Levinger," she said. "I have no idea what he's being charged with, and no one of course has any way of knowing if any of the suspects are guilty of what they will be charged with. Maybe I shouldn't have said what I did about leadership positions. Maybe I should even ask for Rabbi Levinger's forgiveness? It has all come as a real shock." In the end, she said that her council's position was that, if the charges proved true, then the persons who had carried out the terrorist acts deserved condemnation.

Most Israelis, and most settlers, seem to believe that the arrests of the settlers will not substantially slow the process of settlement. The rate of settlement by those Jews ideologically committed to the Land of Israel, who comprised the majority of the settlers during the first fifteen years after the Six-Day War, began to decrease even before the arrests; most of those in Israel who were ready to move into a hostile environment for reasons of belief seem already to have done so. But the rate of settlement into the larger towns such as Ma'aleh Adumim and Ariel—which are populated not by ideological settlers but by Jews seeking, for the most part, a better life—appears to be steady, and will probably not be affected significantly by the crisis among the Gush Emunim and their present and former allies. Whether that crisis and its attendant rifts will continue to plague the ideological settlers will probably depend, to some degree, on the ability of those settlers to develop, and believe in, a new leadership not tainted by the kinds of excesses attributed to the old one. There are enough critics of the old leadership within the Gush Emunim itself to suggest that the emergence of a new leadership is not only possible but likely. And, if one does emerge, it will probably learn something from the *yisurim*, the suffering, that was experienced by the old leadership, and in other ways by Israel as a whole, because of the violent detour that some of the settlers took in their effort to gain possession of the Land of Israel.

I Won't Be the Cossack
of Rabbi Levinger!

I interrupted my interviews in the West Bank to spend a weekend in Modi'in. Modi'in is halfway between Jerusalem and Tel Aviv, within the borders of pre-1967 Israel. Two thousand years ago it was the place where the Maccabees began their revolt against the Syrian Greeks. Now it's the site of Moshav Modi'in, the village established by Shlomo Carlebach.

Carlebach was born in Germany to a family of distinguished scholars and religious leaders. His grandfather, Solomon, was for fifty years the rabbi of the German city of Lübeck. Of Solomon's numerous children and grandchildren, many became well-known rabbis—in Bremen, Cologne, Leipzig, Berlin, New York, Montreal, London, Belfast, Manchester, Jerusalem, Detroit, Newark. One, Shlomo's uncle, was probably the model for the rabbi in Thomas Mann's *Dr. Faustus*. A cousin founded and edited the main mass-circulation Israeli newpapers, *Yediot Aharonot* and *Ma'ariv*. Another cousin was a justice of the Israeli Supreme Court.

Shlomo Carlebach himself came to be known as the "singing rabbi." A man of true musical gifts, he composed melodies derived from the Hasidic tradition and sang them in concerts for large and admiring audiences in the United States, Europe, and Israel. Young Jews who knew nothing of their religious heritage were drawn to him and impressed by him, especially during the late 1960s and early 1970s, when he opened his House of Love and Prayer, in San Francisco. Hippies who had escaped their middle-class, secular, assimilated Jewish origins somehow found their way there and discovered a figure who spoke their language and sang their songs, but who turned that language and song in religious, spiritual, mystical, Hasidic directions. Some retained elements of their hippie styles but combined them, in an original and curious amalgam, with traditional orthodox features: hippie beards with Hasidic earlocks; large yarmulkes embroidered in bright colors; long-sleeved, modest dresses made of Madras cotton rather than Brooklyn polyester.

Some of these former hippies, and others, many of them *ba'alei teshuvah* (a term meaning, literally, "masters of the return," used for irreligious Jews who become religious), followed Carlebach when he established his communal village in Modi'in. Still speaking English, but living in the landscape of the Maccabees, they began to work the rocky soil and to establish a health-food factory. The community is still struggling, and its inhabitants have not fully adjusted to the landscape or the tasks; but they persist in their quest, started in other places, for spirituality, which they get whenever they can from one another and their rabbi. Carlebach is at Modi'in during the summer months and spends the sabbaths, as he did the sabbath I was there, with his wounded and uplifted flock, eating with them, praying with them, learning with them, singing with them.

Also there as visitors that sabbath were a friend who had suggested I come to experience the place—an American sociologist who had visited before—and a friend of that friend, an Israeli-born political scientist. The Israeli, Yaron Ezrahi, forty-three, had studied at Harvard and was a professor at the Hebrew University in Jerusalem; he was also a member of Peace Now, the Israeli organization that has been most active in the search for an Arab–Israeli accommodation and that favors the creation of a Palestinian state in the West Bank.

The sabbath meals at Modi'in are served communally in a

large dining room. The food, vegetarian, was simple but offered with generosity. Every course was followed by melodies composed and led by Rabbi Carlebach; the residents swayed to their repetitive strains, some seemingly transported to other, more celestial, spheres.

The other guests and I, seated together at one of the dining room's long tables, quietly talked about our respective lives and interests. Asked by Yaron Ezrahi what I had been doing on my trip, I explained that I had been visiting the West Bank. Why? he asked. To interview the Arabs and the Jewish settlers, I said.

"The settlers! They're destroying Israel! They're destroying my dream!"

That and more at a high pitch during a soft moment of a tender song. The others in the dining room looked at us and at each other and sang on. Ezrahi continued, more restrained but still in a rage: "The Gush Emunim want me and those I love to spill our blood so that they can realize their fanatic visions of a Land of Israel! You say you saw Rabbi Levinger? He's the biggest fanatic of them all! He wants us to be his cossacks. We should always be on guard, always at war with our Arab neighbors, always suppressing them and making them hate us, so that he can live in his beloved Hebron. I won't be the cossack of Rabbi Levinger!"

Rabbi Carlebach stopped the singing and, not looking directly at us, complained that the vibes weren't good. Here was a holy congregation trying to reach the most awesome heights of heaven, and there were some in its midst pulling it down. It was *mamish*, really, a shame.

Ezrahi knew enough to contain his rage, and I knew enough to arrange another time, on another day, to tap it again.

═══════════

The next week, in his office at the Hebrew University, Ezrahi and I met again, together with Yoram Ben-Porath, an economist. Like Ezrahi, Ben-Porath, forty-six, was born in

Israel. Like Ezrahi he was married and had three children. And like Ezrahi he had been educated in the United States, was a professor at the Hebrew University, and was a member of Peace Now.

For years Ben-Porath had devoted much of his time to the task of persuading his fellow Israelis to risk giving up the occupied territories—the West Bank and Gaza—for peace. And it was about that effort, and how important both he and Ezrahi felt it was, that we talked.

A large percentage of the Israeli population, perhaps 50 percent, according to Ben-Porath, would be willing to trade the territories for peace. "I cannot say that we are the spokesmen for these 50 percent, but it gives you an idea of the support that exists for our position. At the time of the Sabra and Shatilla massacres, Peace Now's general line attracted greater support. On the other hand, if we demonstrate in Hebron against the settlements, such people might criticize us, despite their sympathies for us, for going into an Arab city and demonstrating against Israeli policies in such a way. That is, they might criticize our tactics in one instance or another. I think we speak for approximately 25 to 30 percent of the Israeli people, and another 25 percent of the people might be sympathetic but partly critical—with the criticism that we divide the nation, that we help our enemy. There was always a risk that we could be seen as a leftist fringe group."

Yaron Ezrahi laughed. "My diagnosis in the last few years has been that we don't have a lunatic fringe but a lunatic center!"

What had turned Ben-Porath into a dove, he explained, was the 1967 war. "I realized then that for the first time we had options for peace. Until then it seemed that we were doomed to have peace or war depending on what the other side wanted—though, to be sure, now we know that there *were* a few openings during those years. But after the 1967 war there was a new reality, real choices. This doesn't mean, of course, that it all depends on us. But at least we hold many of the cards. At least now we can think of the Palestinians as a separate issue—separate from the seven Arab countries that, we were always being told, wanted to wipe us out.

"Also, I began to think after the 1967 war of what I wanted to see in a Jewish state. And also I began to put myself in the Arabs' shoes. This doesn't mean that I agree with them, or see us the way they see us. But it does mean that I don't want to deny them the kinds of rights and aspirations that I also consider to be my own."

Ben-Porath was the first person I had encountered during my visit, either Israeli or Arab, who spoke about putting himself in the shoes of his opponent. "There are a few Israelis," I said, "who, like you, can put themselves in the Arabs' shoes. But if you ask an Arab to do the opposite, the request seems to strike him as preposterous. Why do you think that capacity hasn't developed among the Palestinians? For example, they insist that they can't understand the Israelis' fear of the Arabs' intentions to wipe out Israel, because Israel is so strong, and therefore can't understand why they should offer Israel recognition for the purpose of eradicating that fear."

Ben-Porath smiled a historical smile. "The ability of nations in conflict to step into each other's shoes is something new. Even in the French-German conflict I don't think you could have found that—maybe you could have in an isolated case, in the case of an intellectual here or a writer there, but not in the general population. So this is really too big a step to ask from the Palestinians.

"I think that the culture of the Palestinian experience of 1948 makes them feel themselves to be our victims. And this makes them unable to feel our fears. Of course we Jews come to this point in our history with as deep a feeling of victimization as they—probably deeper. And I think that what we see here, then, are two groups with long histories of victimization; and the result is that each side is unable to see the other's experience of victimization, each side is unable to exaggerate the power or cruelty of the other side, and each side is too easily able to justify what it does to the other side on the grounds that it is a victim, it faces great danger, it has to do what is necessary, and anyone who complains about that is simply naive.

"I would say that 80 to 90 percent of the hawkish sentiments among Israelis are based not on aggressive designs and not on biblical beliefs, but rather on the fear of what the Arabs might do. The typical question that goes through the mind of the Israeli is 'What would the Arabs have done to us if they had been in our position—if they had won?' And the typical, unanimous answer is 'They would have destroyed us.' And this is the source of the fear. The Arab inability to understand this is the result of their own sense of victimization; I can't see any other explanation for it. I don't think that the Arabs understand the degree to which their image in the eyes of the Israelis has been colored by their acts of terrorism; but it's precisely on those acts, on the murders of the kids in Maalot and of the people in Nahariya, that Israeli fears—and therefore Israeli hawkishness and Israeli inability to sympathize with Palestinian national aspirations—are based. I don't think the Palestinians understand that. They see them only as excuses."

Ezrahi took up the theme. "It's precisely because there is no Arab counterpart to Peace Now that we were forced to take on their role. My main concern is, how am I going to shape the reality over which I have control? Take the issue of 'Jewish exceptionalism'—the doctrine that Israel should subscribe to a higher morality than the one to which other countries subscribe. We can't become just like any other country—like, say, the French."

It isn't just the Palestinians' inability to put themselves in the shoes of Israelis that makes it difficult for them to engage Israel in negotiation, Ben-Porath observed; they're also caught in their own web of constraints. What does the Palestinian charter say, they ask themselves, about this position or that? What does the latest resolution of the Palestine National Council say? Is it kosher to talk in this way or that about the Jews or Israel? What would the Palestinians outside the West Bank say? Their explanations, Ben-Porath added, seem so "Talmudic." It's really sad to see.

But he said he understood to an extent why the West Bank Palestinians were so constrained by the PLO line. "The Palestinians feel that their only achievement is that they have gained a spokesman in the PLO, a representative, a government-in-exile. So there's a high premium on being consistent with the outside. Besides, the PLO itself is a coalition of various opinions. So it's not just a question of whether the PLO said something. It's also a question of *who* in the PLO said it. People don't want to take risks. Why say something that might be denounced?"

Ezrahi went further. "You know, the phenomenon of the West Bank Palestinians being afraid to contradict the position of the PLO is analogous to a phenomenon experienced by the Jews in America and elsewhere, the phenomenon of their being afraid to contradict the views of the State of Israel. American Jews justify this by saying, 'The Israelis are on the front lines, they are paying the price; we have no right to publicly undercut them even if we disagree with them. When there's a change in Israeli leadership, they'll be more responsive to us. We'll have to wait until then.'

"Regarding the PLO position," Ezrahi continued, "it's based on the Palestinian charter and various Palestine National Council resolutions. Now those are very problematic documents for us. But for the Palestinians they represent the equivalent of a government. And to shift away from the positions expressed in those documents would pose a great risk—the risk of unraveling the PLO position. And so the risk would have to be worth it for the Palestinians to be willing to take it; the possible gain from taking that risk would have to be very great. And to ask them to take that risk without any likely gain would be unfair."

Peace Now advocates Israeli withdrawal from the West Bank and Gaza, and many of its members advocate the establishment in those areas of a Palestinian state. I asked Ben-Porath and Ezrahi about the nightmare expressed to me by many Israelis, of the rise of a Palestinian state whose aim it would be to liberate the rest of Palestine, which is to say Israel itself.

"I assume," Ben-Porath responded, "that the creation of a

Palestinian state would occur under a tremendous asymmetry of power. Israel would be much stronger than it. Also, Palestinians themselves aren't sure what form such a state would take, especially in this first stage. Who would run it? Jordan? The PLO? The extremists? The traditional West Bank forces? My assumption is that Israel would be so strong that either the knowledge of that strength would serve to dampen the possibilities of Arab violence or Israel would have to actually respond to the violence if it arose. I cannot see that the Palestinian state would be a real threat."

Ben-Porath said that he favored Jordanian involvement in any settlement—probably a confederation of that state with the Palestinian one in the West Bank—because such an arrangement would provide a national structure within which Palestinian pressures could be absorbed in relatively peaceful ways, or at least in ways that might not be directed against Israel. And, he added, Jordan had a good record of being able to control anti-Israel forces within it when it feared that the expression of such forces would provoke Israeli retaliation against it. "It would be completely wild for me to guess what the internal dynamics would be of a completely Palestinian state. But I'm thinking in any case of an Israel that would negotiate the giving away of the West Bank from a position of great strength. And its main insurance would be the simple fact that it could reverse its actions."

For the first time in the conversation I felt that Ben-Porath was making the kind of self-assured assumption that no one could be sure of. After all, what if the nightmare of the Israelis really came to pass? What if, after a Palestinian state had been established, even one federated with Jordan, PLO fighters came in from their bases in the Arab world—fighters who, together with their families, had grown up in the venomous conditions of the refugee camps in Syria, Lebanon, and Jordan, and had emerged from those camps with Kalashnikovs in their hands and the dream in their hearts of liberating all of pre-1948 Palestine? What if, after a few years of shaky statehood, after the infrastructure of the Palestinian state had been established,

those fighters, who had grown up waiting to liberate Jaffa and
Haifa because that was where their parents had been born,
began to exert pressure on the government of their state to help
them do the job? What if that government agreed? Or what if it
didn't, fearing Israeli retaliation, and the fighters decided to
take matters into their own hands? What if such fedayeen began to cross the long border into Israel and to blow up schools
and buses? What if Israeli retaliatory strikes did no good because the Palestinian state's government simply couldn't control the fedayeen—who were, after all, pursuing a goal that
for two generations had been declared the most holy goal of
all? What if the attacks continued and escalated? What if a hundred Israelis were killed every month? Three hundred? Five
hundred?

What would Israel do at such a point? What *could* it do?
Certainly it couldn't do what it did in 1967; it couldn't do what
Ben-Porath somehow assumed it would be able to do. It
couldn't just say to the United States and the world: "Sorry.
This is what we told you would happen if we gave up the West
Bank. And now it's happened; now you see the terrible consequences of your ill-considered advice. Now even you have to
admit that the experiment has failed and that we have to act to
protect ourselves. And now even you have to agree that all
that's left for us to do is to retake the West Bank and keep it
forever." It wouldn't be able to say that, and wouldn't be able
to do that, because no one would let it. By that time, after all,
the West Bank would no longer be a disputed territory, as it
was in 1967. It would be a full-fledged state, a member of the
UN. And these days a state, especially if it's not a superpower,
can't just take over another state, certainly not in a permanent
way. No country, not even the United States, would allow that.
The option would simply be unavailable. And the Israeli nightmare would never end. Better, then, if you are an Israeli who
believes that that nightmare can become reality, not to give it a
chance to do so. Better to hold on to the West Bank.

What would you say, I asked Ben-Porath, if Israel gave up
the West Bank, the nightmare turned into reality, and fellow

Israelis came to you, a decade or two from now, and asked how you could have dared lead Israel to such a tragedy by advocating the very circumstances that made that tragedy happen? Would you just say that it was a noble experiment that had failed?

Ben-Porath smiled. "I would say then what I'm saying now. I'm saying now that the risks of staying on the course we are following are greater than the risks of allowing the establishment of a Palestinian state. I don't want twenty years from now to see here a South Africa—a dual society in which different sets of norms exist for Jews and Arabs, and all for the great fun of visiting Shiloh and Hebron, and of speaking about the values that our forefathers bequeathed to us. And that's the *best* scenario I can envision for the situation twenty years from now—a docile Arab population unequal in rights. But I can envision a worse scenario. I can envision a scenario in which there is terror, even under occupation. Riots. Killings every day. And then Israelis will say to each other, 'Jews have to do this or that. It's not pleasant, but the situation requires it. There have to be mass jailings. There have to be collective punishments. We don't like it, but we have to do it.' So here I am again, a grandfather, seeing my children and grandchildren becoming the keepers of the population of the West Bank. So within the set of possible scenarios, and the probabilities that you can attach to them, I'm saying that you have to make a choice; and returning the West Bank is my choice.

"Let me add something else. If Israel continues to hold on to the West Bank, it will be affected internally—it will become less democratic. And it will be less accepted, both by its own people and by others."

As for the Jewish settlements in the West Bank, Ben-Porath told me that no more should be built and that the status of the ones that now exist should be negotiated in the process of establishing the Palestinian state. His own view was that whereas Jews should have the right to live anywhere in the world, particularly in the classical Land of Israel, he didn't think it was good for them to live among Arabs. "I don't think it's useful, at least now. Maybe, after we live side by side for a while with the Arabs, it will become useful; but it isn't now."

Ezrahi broke in: "No one can say that Israelis have the right to settle in the West Bank and in the same breath say that the Palestinians *don't* have the right to settle near Tel Aviv. And if anyone says that the Palestinians *do* have that right, then he's saying that he is not averse to the notion of a binational state."

What about the platform of the Tehiya Party—the platform described to me by Yisrael Medad—which would give Arabs in an annexed West Bank full political rights, including the right to vote, if they accepted Israel as a Jewish state and did national service?

"It seems to me," Ben-Porath answered, "that such plans and offers are not really sincere. From talking to them—from having genuine discussions with them—my conclusion has been that what drives the Gush Emunim is religion, and that they produce these plans regarding the equality that the Arabs would have if they did national service and so on because they don't believe that such a situation will come to pass and because it's useful to say that for export—to answer those foreigners who come to complain about the problem of Arab rights. I don't take those positions seriously. I don't mean to say, by any means, that they are bad people. On the contrary, there are good guys among them, and I see the agony in them when they're faced with the conflict between what they want to do with regard to the Arabs and the human values that they hold in general."

Ezrahi returned to the theme he had introduced during our dinner conversation in Modi'in the week before, but this time without the rage. "Some of those settlers, those religious mystics, sound so reasonable. But when you listen to them you realize that what they want to fight for is really an inconceivable religious utopia. When they realize that that's the program they're fighting for, they shift the ground of the discussion to another field—the field of survival. But that's not really what they're arguing for. They're arguing for a program that's inherently religious, a religious utopia. But the cost of that utopia is

just unacceptable. The military costs alone to achieve that utopia for them would be just incredible."

And, Ben-Porath added, that utopia probably could never
even be realized. "The most likely outcome of this process will
be something incomplete: there will be too many settlements to
dismantle, but not enough, and not well enough developed, to
constitute the religious utopia that the settlers are yearning for.
It will be a permanent mess in which no one will be happy."

But isn't it possible that the mess has already been created?
That the point of no return has already been reached?

"It's possible," Ben-Porath conceded, "or, if not, then we're
probably not very far from it. I don't feel that we're already
past the point of irreversibility, but I think we could be in
several years. But even at that point the annexationists won't
have what they want—a Jewish West Bank. And yet it will be
too late to reverse the process and give up the West Bank in
exchange for peace."

We had been talking about the settlers as if they were all
members of the Gush Emunim, and I described the many I had
met who were not religious at all. I described, for example, the
taxi driver who had taken me one day to Shiloh. His parents
had been killed during Arab riots in Hebron. He had moved,
however, not to Hebron but to Ma'aleh Adumim, a bedroom
suburb between Jerusalem and Jericho. He had moved there
not because he felt it was a holy act to settle in the Land of
Israel but because it was cheaper to live in Ma'aleh Adumim
than in Jerusalem; he was able to sell his home in Jerusalem,
buy a much larger one in Ma'aleh Adumim for much less money, and invest the difference. While I was examining the archaeological digs of the first capital of Israel, he was searching the
area to find old-looking rocks that he could set in the garden of
his new West Bank town house.

I also described Ya'akov Fitelson, the mayor of Ariel, an
energetic Jewish émigré from the Soviet Union who had outlined, to me and reporters from the United States, his optimistic
plans for the town. He said that Ariel would first be a suburb of
Tel Aviv, since it was just a few minutes' driving time from that

city. Then it would grow to become a Tel Aviv itself, rivaling it
in size and attracting to itself new high-technology industries.
And then it would start to develop its own suburbs, stretching
much of the way to Nablus.

Ben-Porath listened and nodded in sad agreement. "This is
the Meron Benvenisti argument. If the West Bank settler population becomes large enough because it attracts large numbers
of such non-ideological settlers—if it becomes an important
part of Israeli life because, say, the only way you can get an
apartment for your newly married children that you can afford
is by getting one for them in Ariel—then the process of Jewish
settlement in the West Bank will be truly irreversible."

Ezrahi returned to the aspirations of the Gush Emunim and
to the price that Israelis would have to pay in order to realize
them. "I want to tell you about a relative of my wife's from
Kibbutz Ein Shemer. She lost her husband in the 1967 war, in
the battle for Ammunition Hill. She raised her three children by
herself. Two children are in the army. One of them served in
Lebanon. Now, the 1967 war was a war of survival. We saw it
as such; it was a war in which we could have been destroyed. I
want one of those guys from Gush Emunim to sit in front of
this woman and tell her that that war was a *ness*, a miracle
[designed by God to deliver the West Bank into the hands of the
Jews]—that war in which her husband was killed! And I want
him to tell her that we'll have another *ness*, another miracle,
in which she'll lose a child! And from *ness* to *ness*," Ezrahi
laughed bitterly, "we'll get into a mess!"

"You know something?" he added angrily. "I don't mind if
these people live by their faith in their miracles so long as my
blood isn't the instrument by which they realize those miracles!
That's all! And it's as raw and down-to-earth as that. I have no
tolerance for people whose miracles involve direct threats to the
lives of people I know." And here Ezrahi, slashing the air between us with his open hand, repeated what he had said to me
at Modi'in the previous week: "I don't want the people I love
to become the cossacks of Rabbi Levinger! He will sit there on
his hill with all of his fantasies, and thousands of our youth will

die to realize them! This is some kind of pathology!"

Ben-Porath, seeing our conversation come to its end, turned once again to the question of the irreversibility of the Jewish settlement process in the West Bank. "I don't think it's too late," he said, smiling. "I'm generally pessimistic, but there's great intellectual arrogance in pessimism. My ability, and our collective ability, to predict the future is poor. And all the people who are saying with absolute assurance that the process of settlement in the West Bank is irreversible are committing the same act of intellectual arrogance. There are so many ways in which things can reverse themselves. History is erratic and unpredictable—it was in the past and continues to be. In fact, there's reason here for optimism. After so long a period of occupation half of the Israeli population is still against annexation! This is a tribute to the Jewish people and to their moderation. Where else in the world would a people behave in the same way? Where else in the world would a people with claims to a land, and with the belief that relinquishing that land would pose a mortal threat to their survival, nevertheless still consider relinquishing it?"

Ben-Porath was pleased with his rhetorical question. A Jew who found the policies of the Likud government and the Gush Emunim in violation of his concepts of traditional Jewish decency and justice, he was still able to find in the attitudes of most Israelis a vibrant representation of that Jewishness. He asked me to be sure to quote the question, and to note his pride in the conclusion about Israel that it implied.

The Crisis within Israel: Demography Democracy and the Kahane Factor

Umm al-Fahm, an Arab village in northern Israel, is built on hills overlooking the Wadi Ara road. More than 3,000 years ago, before the children of Israel entered the Promised Land, that road was an already-ancient mountain pass that carried armies from Egypt toward Mesopotamia and back. Over the millennia it was the site of numerous battles and ambushes, with forces occupying the heights above usually destroying the invaders below. Sometimes, by stealth and daring, the invaders surprised their foes and routed them in battles of biblical dimension.

In the summer of 1984, Meir Kahane, just elected to the Israeli Knesset, vowed to become the road's newest invader. His goal, he said, was to open an Arab emigration office in Umm al-Fahm. The villagers, all citizens of Israel, vowed, for their part, to stop him. The confrontation promised to be the most dramatic challenge yet to the integrity and survival of Israeli democracy.

For many of Kahane's Israeli critics, he was just a "stray weed" in Israeli politics, a racist extremist who represented no more than the 26,000 Israelis who had endorsed him – merely 1.3 percent of the electorate, just over the minimum one percent required to win a Knesset seat. But even those voters, his critics added, had given Kahane their support primarily to send a message of angry rejection to the country's established politicians. The majority of them, these critics explained, did not agree with Kahane's calls for the expulsion of Israel's Arabs, as well as the Arabs of the West Bank and Gaza, just as they did not agree with his calls for laws against sexual relations between Arabs and Jews or the establishment of a theocracy based on his fundamentalist version of Jewish law.

Other Israelis, however, feared that Kahane's election was in fact an accurate, and ominous sign of a serious deterioration in the health of Israeli democracy. He was, they said, no stray weed. The decades of unrelenting Arab hostility and the country's increasing international isolation were, they argued, beginning to fray the fabric of Israel's national democratic consensus. Internal divisions, which had always existed, were growing sharper. Differences between many Jewish groups – between religious Jews and non-religious Jews, between those of Oriental, or Sephardi, origin and those of Western, or Ashkenazi, origin, and between those on the political left and those on the right – were taking on the character of strife rather than healthy debate. As the country's economy has worsened, as foreign criticism has increased, and as other pressures have grown, intolerance has become more prominent, and those whose views are different from one's own have been seen increasingly as enemies, even traitors, rather than as participants in the national political discussion. Kahane's railings against the Arabs, the Israeli left, non-religious Jews and Western values were attracting a genuine, if still small, following among the most polarized and frustrated sectors of the population. And, these apprehensive Israelis warned, if that following continued to grow, and if many other Israelis joined the flight into extremisms of one sort or another, then Israel's political life would lose its broad center, the country would become radicalized, the trust necessary to maintain civil compromise would be damaged, and the democratic traditions and institutions in which Israelis have for so long prided themselves would be threatened.

And, more than that, the country's very existence would be threatened. If it lost its character as a democratic state, these

Israelis predicted, it would probably also lose its main friend in the international arena, the United States, whose government and people have long supported it and wished it well because the democratic values to which it subscribed were the same as theirs, and because those values made it a stable and reliable ally in an otherwise unpredictable and autocratic corner of the world. With all that at stake, these Israelis concluded, Kahane's sudden and striking electoral success betokened something very ominous indeed for the future of the Jewish state. Small wonder, they added wryly, that Kahane had received more than a few votes among the country's Arab population.

═══════

That Kahane chose to invade Umm al-Fahm – where he would, as he put it, "make the Arabs an offer to leave the country they couldn't refuse" – was no accident.

First of all, the village had been, for more than a decade, the main center for some of the most radical Arab groups in Israel. One such group, the Ibn al-Balad, or Sons of the Village, has repeatedly held strikes to protest Israeli policies. And other groups, operating secretly and reportedly linked to the PLO, have been subjected to crackdowns and arrests for storing caches of weapons to be used in terrorist attacks.

But there was another and far more important reason that Kahane chose Umm al-Fahm as the target of his post-election invasion. In 1949, when the village became part of the newly created Jewish state, it had a population of 3,200. In the 36 years since then, the figure has grown to 24,000. This enormous jump – a nearly sevenfold increase – has been seen by some Israeli Jews as emblematic of the population explosion that has been experienced by Israel's Arab minority. Numbering only 156,000 in 1949, that minority now totals 700,000, with the increase due almost solely to the Arabs' high fertility rate. Given the fact that their fertility rate is nearly double that of the Jews, it appears, according to some Israeli demographers, that the Arabs, who are now about 17 percent of the country's population of 4.2 million, may, in 30 years, be 24 percent.

According to Kahane, however, that estimate is low. He insists that, by the middle of the next century, the percentage of Israelis who are Arabs will be much higher than the experts predict. By then, he says, the Arabs will be unified, control a plurality if not a majority of the vote, and use the power of the ballot to dismantle the underpinnings of the Jewish state – especially the Law of Return, passed by the Knesset in 1950, five years after the Holocaust, which gives every Jew everywhere the right to automatic haven in Israel. With their votes, the Israeli Arabs could revoke that law, revise the Declaration of Independence, which identifies Israel as a Jewish state, and even change the name of the country to Palestine. In this process, carried out solely through democratic means, Israel would cease to exist, the Jews would no longer have a national home, and Jews being persecuted in other countries would once again have nowhere to flee.

But as unsettling as this demographic nightmare is to many Israeli Jews, Kahane adds a coda designed to unsettle them even more. The Arabs of the West Bank and Gaza, he says, who now number 1.2 million, must also be included in these calculations. Though not citizens of Israel now, they could become citizens if those territories are, as he and other Israelis believe they should be, annexed. Should that happen, then Israel's Arab population would suddenly constitute about 35 percent of the total, and, within just 30 years, according to the predictions of even the most conservative demographers, it would amount to well over half. If these Arabs, too, are given citizenship, they could, even more quickly than the current Israeli Arabs acting alone, dismantle the Jewish state.

What Kahane concludes from this demographic nightmare is that Israel cannot be both a democratic and a Jewish state. If it remains democratic, and Arabs can vote, then it will eventually stop being Jewish. Since for him the Jewish nature of the state is more important than its democratic nature, the latter must be abandoned in favor of the former. The Arabs, he argues, must be "transferred" from the country, both from Israel proper and from the occupied territories. They must be encouraged to leave through financial incentives and other means, including intimidation; and those who choose to stay must no longer have the right to vote.

———————

On the morning of August 29, 1984, the day on which, Kahane had announced, he would invade Umm al-Fahm, thousands of arngry Arab residents were waiting to confront him in the village. Nor were they alone. The previous night, several hundred Israeli Jews had arrived to give the village their moral support; and, that morning, a dozen members of the 120-member Knesset, most of them Jews, had arrived to do the same thing. Hundreds more Israeli Jews had come that morning to give their support, but, unlike the Knesset members, were not allowed entry into the village. The police, a thousand strong, considered the situation extremely dangerous. Unable to stop Kahane because of his newly-won shield of parliamentary immunity, they expected the worst, and had orders to keep all outsiders, whether supporters of the villagers or of Kahane, out. The Wadi Ara road below the village soon filled with Jews, many wearing facsimiles of the yellow Star of David that the Nazis had forced Jews to wear in European ghettos and concentration camps, each star inscribed, in Hebrew, with the words, "We Will Not Let Racism Pass."

Trying to enter Umm al-Fahm that morning as well, I approached the police officer on the road, asking to be allowed into the village. He refused. After I pressed him again, he grew agitated, warning that anything could happen, that tempers were so high an explosion might take place, that no more persons could be let in, even journalists, and that if I pressed him any further, and distracted him from the task of keeping order, he would be forced to arrest me. Suddenly, down the road, I saw a group of Jews bolt across a field and up a hillside. I followed, quickly climbing the hills above the ancient pass. Soon dozens more were climbing, pulling themselves up by the rocks and scrub. We reached the other side, climbed still more hills, and found ourselves, finally, on a bluff overlooking the village entrance below.

===============

Kahane had promised to arrive in Umm al-Fahm at 10 a.m. Three nights before, emigration forms had been placed in the village square together with leaflets saying that Israel was the land of the Jews and that, in order to avoid conflict, the Arabs had to leave. Arabs willing to emigrate to Western countries, the leaflets added, would receive visas, housing and jobs.

Numerous Israelis, from the left of the political spectrum to the right, as well as newspapers and organizations, urged the Interior Minister, Yosef Burg, who was in charge of the police, to bar Kahane's entry into the village. Burg, however, argued that the principle of parliamentary immunity is an important one and should not be suspended arbitrarily. Victor Shemtov, a Knesset member and the leader of the left-wing Mapam Party, then a partner in Shimon Peres's Labor Alignment, sent Burg a telegram asking him to prevent the visit, which, he warned, was "of a provocative nature," and "apt to lead to serious incidents"; allowing Kahane's followers into the town, he warned, might start "things that no one knows how they will end." Burg held firm. A local police commander warned the Umm al-Fahm council that "if one stone is thrown at Kahane, the entire council will be held responsible." Earlier that month, the head of the council, Hashem Mahamid, predicted that, were Kahane to be allowed into Umm al-Fahm, the residents of the village would respond by stoning him. On the day before the visit Mahamid added that, if any violence were to take place, it would be Burg, not the council, who would be responsible.

On the Wadi Ara road that morning, the commander of the northern police district, Rahamim Hadad, a Jew of Oriental origin, had a telephone line open to the Israeli Police Inspector-General, Arye Ivtzan, who was, in turn, in touch with Burg. Within the village itself, the tension mounted. Residents and their Jewish supporters, facing a barricade of policemen, chanted "Jewish-Arab brotherhood!" and "Fascism won't pass!" Above them, on a barren hillside, many more watched, climbing up and down, as if aimlessly, with an increasing frequency that matched their increasing tension. Suddenly, just before 1:00 in the afternoon, as the police commander drove in from the Wadi Ara road, rumors spread that it was Kahane. Screaming "With our blood and spirit we will redeem you, Umm al-Fahm!" the Arabs surrounding me on the hillside, with whom I had just been talking, youths as well as grown men, hurled stones at the car and the police. The police, in turn, shot volleys of tear gas. We ran further up the hill, our skin burning, enveloped in the acrid, burning smoke. Children passed me sections of onion, which they said would counteract the effects of the gas. An Arab family, seeing me coughing, ushered me into the refuge of its modest house. A woman inside gave me water, and told me she was ready to crush Kahane's skull.

Only later did the villagers learn that, before noon, Kahane had been stopped on the Wadi Ara road just a mile from the village, and that, soon after, he had been forbidden entry into it. The police told Kahane that they would be unable to guarantee his safety. And, they told the press, the situation was by then so dangerous that it threatened state security. Under the circumstances, parliamentary immunity could not be maintained. The police commander's arrival in the village, which had precipitated the first volley of stones, had in fact been for the purpose of informing the villagers that Kahane would not come.

Interviewing the chairman of Umm al-Fahm's village council later that day, I learned that the villagers saw the event as a victory. "A great thing happened today," Hashem Mahamid told me exultantly. "We achieved a unity of Jews and Arabs working together. The first victims of Kahane would be the Arabs, and the next might be the leftists. This is the first line of the history that will be written about the cooperation of Arabs and Jews in fighting such phenomena."

But if the Arabs of Umm al-Fahm saw the day as a victory of Israel's democracy over the efforts by Kahane to destroy it, many anti-Kahanist Israeli Jews saw it in far less hopeful terms. For them, the battle of Umm al-Fahm was not yet over, and was in fact only part of a much greater battle within Israel – a battle not only between Arabs and Jews but, even more powerfully, between Jews and Jews: a battle about the role of religion, about relations between different Jewish ethnic and political groups, and ultimately, about democracy and the future of the Jewish state.

======================

Who is Meir Kahane? How has he come to be able to frighten not only the Arabs of Israel but also the Jews?

The archives of newspapers, both in Israel and the United States, contain volumes of clippings documenting his exploits; their indices are full of references to his clashes with Jews and Arabs, blacks and whites, Jerusalem police and New York police, Soviet officials and Israeli ones. No one considers Kahane an ordinary man, least of all Kahane himself.

Kahane grew up in the Flatbush section of Brooklyn 52 years before his attempt to invade Umm al-Fahm – in the streets, as he put it, learning to live in a rough world in which young Jews with yarmulkes were often beaten and robbed. Bloodied more than once, he learned to fight back, and then to live with – even, he says, to drink beer with – his former tormentors; as soon as the bullies saw he would not be bullied, he believes, they came to respect him.

Kahane's father was an admirer of Vladimir Jabotinsky, the Russian Zionist Revisionist and mentor of Menachem Begin. Kahane's first arrest, in 1947, when he was 15, took place, he recalls, when he helped smash the car of Ernest Bevin as it was coming down the Queen Mary's gangplank in New York; as the British foreign secretary, Bevin had been blocking attempts by Jewish survivors of the Holocaust to enter Palestine, and Kahane considered him an enemy of the Jewish people.

Following his graduation from the Brooklyn Talmudical Academy in 1949, and then Brooklyn College, Kahane studied law and international relations at New York University and obtained rabbinical ordination from the Mirer Yeshiva in New York. After an unsuccessful attempt to settle in Israel, he returned to the United States, was fired from his position as the rabbi of a synagogue in New York City's borough of Queens, and became a journalist, first for the *Brooklyn Daily* and then the Orthodox *Jewish Press.*

While at the latter newspaper, during the mid-60s, Kahane began to lead, as Sol Stern put it in the October 2, 1984, issue of the *Village Voice,* "a double life." Using the name Michael King, he rented an apartment on Manhattan's East side, spent many nights there while his wife and four children remained in Queens, began to attend parties, and left the impression that he was a representative of a foreign wire service, well-connected with the U.S. intelligence apparatus, and, by some accounts, a bachelor and a Christian. It was during this time, in 1966, that the 33-year-old Kahane, according to Michael Kaufman and Richard Severo, two reporters for the New York *Times* who later investigated his past, apparently had a brief affair with Estelle Donna Evans, a 21-year-old Christian woman; soon after Kahane broke off the relationship, Evans jumped off New York City's Queensborough Bridge, was rescued, and died two days later. Sol Stern, in his *Village Voice* article, argues that, despite Kahane's frequent subsequent denials, that affair really did take place, had a profound impact on him, and played both a tragic and ironic role in the life of a married rabbi who would later press for an Israeli law banning sexual relations between Jews and non-Jews. Curiously, in a 1972 *Playboy* interview, Kahane claimed that he had assumed the name Michael King, and had led his double life, as part of an arrangement he had with the FBI to do research on the American radical right.

Later in 1968, this time as Meir Kahane, he founded the Jewish Defense League. His aim, he maintained, was not only to protect the lives of Jews in a period of rising anti-Semitism, but also to change their image from craven victims to self-sufficient equals. In the process, he and his young followers clashed with the city's blacks, whom they accused of preying on helpless, especially elderly, Jews; and, as the Jewish emigration movement grew in the Soviet Union, he added, as targets of his attacks, Soviet officials and property in the United States, as well as Americans doing business with the Soviet Union.

In 1972 Kahane moved his operations to an Israel reluctant to receive him, still shuttling back and forth between the two countries. In 1974 he founded his militant Kach movement in Israel, whose name, meaning "thus," was taken from the motto of the Jewish underground, the Irgun Tz'vai Le'umi, that, under Menachem Begin's leadership, had fought the British in Palestine, sometimes with terrorist tactics: *"Rak kach!* – Only thus!" Running for the Knesset in several elections, Kach failed to win the one percent minimum required for a seat – failed, that is, until the vote in July of 1984.

Altogether, Kahane estimates that he has been arrested "hundreds of times," both in the United States and Israel, and that he has spent more than a month in prison after at least 20 of those arrests. Some of the arrests were for violating probation; some for arms smuggling; some for incitement; and some for entering areas, usually Arab towns and villages, from which he had been banned. The Israeli prisons, he recalls, were always tougher than the American; in America, in fact, where he served a sentence for being involved in a conspiracy to manufacture a bomb, he was able to obtain special treatment and kosher food, while in Israel he was often subjected to harsh conditions. As a result of his election to the Knesset, he won not only a seat but also protection from the police under Israel's laws of parliamentary immunity. Those immunity laws are probably the most far-reaching in the world; they were originally passed to ensure Israeli democracy by guaranteeing that no dissident Knesset member would be restricted in his freedom of speech or action by the power of an arbitrary government.

I met with Kahane, three weeks after his election, in a catering hall of the Plaza Hotel in West Jerusalem. The hall had recently been used, was in disarray, almost totally dark, and, with its air conditioning off, very warm. A small ceiling light barely illuminated the corner table at which we sat.

"I'm convinced," Kahane told me, glancing around the large, empty room, "that there are any number of people in this country who, because of the last two-and-a-half weeks of nonstop hatred and lies, may feel that it's their patriotic duty to assassinate me."

Sitting forward in his chair, the collar of his white shirt spread over the lapels of his suit jacket, Kahane characterized the unremitting post-election attacks on him by a broad spectrum of Israelis – ranging, as it happens, from former Prime Minister Menachem Begin ("I totally reject everything he says") to Jerusalem mayor Teddy Kollek ("a stain on Israeli democracy") – as a kind of McCarthyism typical of liberals: "There is no greater defamer or basic fascist than the liberal, who has an arrogance that transcends his ignorance – the arrogance of assuming that anyone who doesn't agree with him has to be an evil person." But all that criticism, he said – as well as the unprecedented refusal of Israel's President to consult him in the process of attempting to form a government, and the orders given to the staff of the state broadcasting service not to report on him – only serve his ends. "What they're doing for me," he explained, "is what they did for Begin: They're creating in the minds of the underdogs of Israel a champion who is himself an underdog."

Kahane laughed: "Of course that helps me. Of course that helps me." He predicted that, in a new election, people who had not voted for him in previous elections out of the fear that they would be wasting their vote on someone who could not win would finally do so: "I'd get four or five seats without the *slightest* problem. The future *is* mine!" And that future, he added, would be all the more his the more the Israeli media ignored his popularity among the Sephardi Jews and among the young. "They can't stop me and they know it," he went on. "This whole election was a miracle of God. I walked between the raindrops. The only answer is God." It must have been God, Kahane insisted, who saw to it that the effort to remove his party from the ballot was stopped by the Israeli Supreme Court, and it must have been God who saw to it that the effort to censor his election commercials served, instead, to provoke sympathy for his cause. One television commercial that was not censored referred to Jews he said had been murdered by Arabs, and showed drops of blood dripping onto a tiled floor, with a cross-armed Kahane, Jersualem's Temple Mount behind him, saying, "Give me the power and I'll take care of them."

I asked Kahane what he meant by "I'll take care of them."

"I'll take care of them. What's so difficult about understanding that? I have a program in which I call for the transfer of Arabs out of Israel. Give me the power and I'll take care of them by transferring them out of Israel."

"Transferring them – which is another way of saying expulsion?"

"It's another word for throwing them out, it's another word for paying them money – it's for transferring them out of the country any way that they will go. In 1945 the Poles and the Czechs transferred – expelled, threw out – 12 million ethnic Germans from Silesia, the Sudetenland, Danzig and so on. It was ratified at Potsdam; it's part of international law today. Truman, Attlee, Stalin – nobody said anything about that. I have no intention of losing my country to Arab bullets or Arab babies."

Kahane insisted that Peace Now and other Israeli peace groups had arisen in the country only because of Jewish guilt over the dispossession of Arabs as a result of the creation of Israel; and he insisted that the Israelis in those movements, as well as other Israelis on the left, hate him because he makes them feel their guilt all the more by reminding them of a contradiction inherent in their idea of Israel. "Secular, political Zionism," he explained, "came into being to create a Jewish state. A Jewish state means, at the least, a state with a majority of Jews. [The founders of the state] certainly didn't want to create another Brooklyn! On the other hand, the same Zionists babble about democracy. Well, democracy finds it irrelevant whether you're a Jew or not a Jew. So the [Israeli] Declaration of Independence, which is a model of schizophrenia – it's just a magnificent model of it, as were Herzl and Ben-Gurion – says that Israel is a Jewish state with equal political rights for all its citizens. Well," Kahane sneered, "you can't have a *democratic* Jewish state! You can have a democratic state or you can have a Jewish state or you can have an Arab state, but you can't have a *democratic* Jewish state. And I get up and say that and they go crazy because I've touched the most horrible of all sores. They've got to choose: Am I a Western democrat or am I a Zionist?

Kahane is convinced that, in 50 years, the Israeli Arabs will reach majority status in the country as a result of their high birth rate and the rising emigration rate of the Jews. And, if the West Bank and Gaza were annexed, then the Arabs would become a majority population much sooner than that. "That's why," Kahane explained, "I want these people out."

Kahane went on to explain why he is hated by so many Israelis. The right-wing parties hate him, he said, because he threatens to take votes from them. And the left hates him because he makes them face the reality they prefer not to see. The *Jerusalem Post*, he said, like the rest of the left-leaning Israeli press, repeatedly misquotes and excoriates him because what he says reveals the untenability of their beliefs: "What bothers the *Post* is that I challenge them to answer the question, 'Do the Arabs have a right to be the majority in this country?' That's what kills them."

Finally, Kahane dismissed my warning that, were Israel to try to carry out his program – the part of it involving the "transfer" of the Arabs or the denial to them of citizenship in Israel should they wish to remain there – then other nations might react harshly, with disastrous results: "What in the world makes you think there was no outside world in the time of Joshua? What in the world makes you think that the Canaanites didn't have a lot of cousins, and angry cousins, outside of Canaan? What in the world makes you think that somehow in those days there was no outside world that cared? But also my whole program is based on the assumption that God is stronger than Ronald Reagan. If God isn't stronger than Ronald Reagan, I'm in the wrong business. I'm in the wrong faith, the wrong people. I should go back and bury myself in Brooklyn. I believe that when God says in the Torah, 'They are a people that dwells alone, and is not counted among the nations,' that it means something. It either means something or it means nothing.

We're a people, a people with a faith. What does it mean that we're Jews? It's not that we eat kosher. It's that we believe that if we do what He wants that He will save us."

═══════════

During my stay in Israel, other Jews told me, some desperately, that what they wanted most to be saved from is Meir Kahane. That he is dangerous for Israel, and wrong about Judaism, they had no doubt; the main disagreement among them was about the extent of the support he enjoys in the country.

Some insisted that he is just an aberration – that every society has its fringes and its outcasts, and that Kahane and his Kach followers are nothing more than that. The fact that he attracted 1.3 percent of the voters was, they thought, not very significant. What percentage of American voters, they asked, is ready to vote for the Ku Klux Klan or the American Nazi Party or other far-right or far-left fringe groups? Probably far higher than that. And equally extremist and racist parties regularly run for election, and regularly attract a far higher percentage of votes, in other democracies, without it being said of those countries that they are themselves racist or extremist; in fact, the successes of those parties, if noticed at all, are cited as testaments to the democracies that permit them.

Other Israelis, however, told me they fear Kahane is in fact an extreme expression of an increasingly-powerful sentiment among Israeli Jews. One such Israeli, Yehoshafat Harkabi, a professor of international relations at the Hebrew University and formerly chief of Israeli military intelligence, pointed out that, like every religion, especially every religion with ancient roots, Judaism contains many elements, some of them harsh and inconsistent not only with modernity but also with other of its elements. It's possible, he said to me, to point to one or another religious source and justify any action against the Arabs, especially in the light of the fact that Arabs have themselves preached, and even carried out, far more severe actions against the Jews during the centuries when Jews lived under their control – and particularly in the light of the unremitting hostility still focussed by most of the Arab world on Israel, as well as the denial by so many Arabs, including Palestinians, of Israel's right to exist. Under these circumstances, it might be understandable that, now that Jews have sovereignty and power in their own land, some of them might be attracted to an ideology that gives expression to some of their frustrations and resentments.

But that ideology, Harkabi said, is not only wrong; it is a path toward national suicide – especially the part of the ideology that calls for the annexation of the West Bank and Gaza on the grounds that it is the Jews' God-given patrimony. It is that call, he said, that, for obvious demographic reasons, makes Kahane's program for the expulsion of the Arabs seem necessary to some Jews, and it is that call that has given rise to the Jewish terrorist underground now on trial in Israel. This is, Harkbai told me, at its root a religious problem; its solution depends on the willingness of Jewish religious leaders in Israel to face, and dissociate from modern applicability, those elements in ancient scripture that have been resurrected and inaccurately cited, with a vicious and anti-humanist vengeance, by such demagogues as Meir Kahane.

As it happens, some religious Israeli Jews have already taken up theological arms against Kahane and other manifestations of the religious right. Allying themselves to varying degrees with secular Israeli peace movements such as Peace Now, these Jews have, in the past decade, and especially in the last few years, argued energetically that neither Kahane nor the Gush Emunim – the "Bloc of the Faithful" committed to settling the West Bank – can justify their activities on religious grounds. For every quotation from the Bible or the Talmud that Kahane or the Gush have cited to support their respective (and very different) efforts, they have cited others more consistent with the humanist ethos that yearns for peace and harmony between Jews and Arabs; they have insisted that the traditions of Jewish law and learning are overwhelmingly on their side, and against Kahane.

One such group, called Oz VeShalom – Strength and Peace – maintains that the spiritual values that are at the heart of Judaism are more important than any claim to land, however justified historically, and that such a claim cannot be pursued if it damages those values. Yehezkel Landau, the information secretary of the organization – an immigrant from the United States and a former student of psychology and theology at the Harvard Divinity School – told me that his group believes that no theological claim can justify damage done to another people. He believes that the kind of messianism exemplified by Kahane and the Gush Emunim has severely wounded the Jews in the past; that no one can say with any authority or knowledge what God wants or doesn't want in this or any generation; that Judaism views all human beings, including Arabs, as worthy of dignity and respect; that the ancient precepts in Joshua and Numbers regarding the conquest of the Land of Israel have no bearing on modern realities in the area; and that what Israeli Jews must do is seek a political compromise with their Palestinian brothers for sovereignty in the land that is dear to, and home to, them both.

Other members of Oz VeShalom and an allied religious organization, Netivot Shalom (Paths of Peace), expressed similar views in my meetings with them. One, Uriel Simon, a professor of Bible at the Hebrew University, believes that the Jewish religious tradition is above all a tradition of justice and humaneness, that Israel must not inflict on Arabs the kind of indignities that have been inflicted on Jews, and that, for the sake of peace and justice, Israel should permit Palestinian self-determination in the West Bank and Gaza. Another professor, Avi Ravitsky, in a televised debate, challenged Moshe Levinger, the Gush Emunim leader in Hebron who had already criticized Kahane for calling secular Jews *mityavnim,* or assimilated Hellenists, to dissociate himself fully from Kahane, and argued that it was precisely the narrow religious and nationalistic ideologies of Levinger and other Jewish settlers that had fostered the kind of extremism that was finally being exemplified by Kahane and the Jewish terrorist underground.

Still another religious peace activist, Jeremy Milgrom, went even further. A Conservative rabbi in his early 30s – an

immigrant from the United States who was ordained by the
Jewish Theological Seminary in New York – Milgrom has
devoted most of his life to improving Arab-Jewish relations in
Israel. Exquisitely pained by any injustice, especially injustice
by Jews toward Arabs, he does everything he can to foster
understanding between the two communities. At Umm al-Fahm
on the day that Kahane had pledged to come, he was arrested
after attempting to separate the Arabs and the police. Intently,
almost plaintively, he told me that he wants to help right the
wrongs that he feels Arabs have suffered at the hands of Jews,
even if they have been suffered in the process of Arab efforts to
deny the Jews what the Arabs themselves now want – national
self-determination.

Other religious Jews I interviewed, including some religious
authorities, strenuously rejected Kahane's conviction that all
religious Jews would prefer to live in a theocratic rather than a
secular state. One, the 82-year-old Yeshayahu Leibowitz – a
physician and former professor of biochemistry at the Hebrew
University, now a professor of philosophy there and the author
of numerous articles and books on Jewish law and belief –
thundered his insistence that the state was, by its nature, a
secular construct, and should in no way be allowed to take on a
religious character or function. And still others insisted that
Kahane's repeated assertions that his positions and beliefs are
grounded in Jewish law are simply, and mendaciously, wrong.

But my talks with Israelis revealed sharp repudiations of
Kahane by members of yet other segments of the population on
whose allegiance he and less extreme nationalists have laid claim.
While most of Kahane's support has indeed come from the
Oriental Jewish community, especially those from Morocco,
many of the Sephardi Jews I interviewed were appalled by his
beliefs, and insulted that Jews outside Israel, and within it,
automatically associate their communities with Kahanist sympathies. One, Shlomo Elbaz, a professor of French literature at
the Hebrew University, had helped found HaMizrach el
HaShalom, East for Peace, which advocates a Peace Now
position but with a special Oriental Jewish perspective. A

Moroccan-born Jew himself, Elbaz told me that Israelis will have to find their place in the Middle East by being more like the Arabs; with the Oriental Jewish community now a majority in the country, and with Oriental-Western intermarriage now at a level of perhaps 20 percent, Israeli Jews are creating a culture that lies between East and West, one that will hold on to its humanism while retaining the rhythms and texture of life in the Levant. For him, Kahane is not only a stray weed among the Jews, but Kahanism is a stray weed among the Orientals – stray and without a real future.

Yet another Moroccan-born Israeli I interviewed, Dede Ben-Shitrit – not a light-skinned, refined professor like Elbaz but a dark Moroccan Jew of lower-class origins who had become a member of the Jerusalem Municipal Council because of his organizing activities at the neighborhood level – indicated that the poor Oriental Jews are not, at heart, fertile soil for the kind of vegetation that Kahane's ideas represent, and are perhaps more ready for accommodation with the Arabs, and less fearful of them, than are their Ashkenazi counterparts.

In addition, one recent survey of a group said to be strongly sympathetic to Kahane has revealed just the opposite. The group – surveyed in 1983 and composed of 100 American Jewish immigrants who have moved to 40 West Bank settlements – were found by Haim Waxman of Rutgers University to subscribe to American democratic and liberal political and social values, and to "by and large strongly reject" Meir Kahane and his views.

And, in the Knesset itself, efforts have been made to curb, and even stop, Kahane. During a debate four months after he was elected, one parliamentarian, a Liberal Party member in the right-wing Likud coalition, called Kahane "a cancer in the body politic," and proposed that the Kach Party, "and any party that strikes at the foundations of the state's existence," be outlawed. Another member of the Likud, belonging to Menachem Begin's Herut Party, denounced as racist, and similar to Hitler's Nuremberg Laws, two bills Kahane had circulated that would make it a criminal offense for Jews to have sexual relations with non-Jews, that would forbid non-Jews from living within the boundaries of Jerusalem, and that would provide for separate schools, summer camps and beaches for Jews and Arabs. Later, Israel's Attorney General, Yitzhak Zamir, attacked Kahanism as a shameful, loathsome and dangerous phenomenon that is opposed to Jewish tradition, international law and the principles of Zionism, and is more dangerous for Israel's Jews than for its Arabs. Zamir made public two Knesset proposals. One was to establish a Basic Law that would bar from a general election any party that opposes the existence of Israel as a state, that opposes its democratic system of government or that supports racism. Another was to authorize the police, for a period of a year, to prevent Kahane from entering any Arab settlement, or any factory that employs a majority of Arab workers, if he announces such an intention in advance.

On December 25, 1984, by a secret vote of 58 to 36, the Knesset did indeed limit Kahane's parliamentary immunity by barring his entry into Israeli Arab villages such as Umm al-Fahm. The split vote did not necessarily reflect the full extent of opposition to Kahane within the Knesset itself. Despite their strong anti-Kahane sentiments, some Knesset members, like many Israelis, oppose the efforts to limit Kahane's immunity or to pass other laws aimed at restricting his freedom of action; they fear that such restrictions could create dangerous, anti-democratic precedents that might later be applied to others with unpopular views. But they, and many other Israelis, have repeatedly taken to the streets against Kahane, with one Tel Aviv demonstration in November of 1984 drawing several thousand Israeli youth. Yet despite the split vote on the anti-Kahane resolution, there was in the Knesset a unity of sentiment against Kahane that is rarely evident in that very contentious body. In presenting the resolution, the chairman of the Knesset committee that had drafted and passed it, Micha Reiser, a Likud Party member, said he knew of no issue that had so coalesced the Knesset: "No political party, from Tehiya [on the right] to the Communists, has concealed its dissociation from, and even disgust" with Kahane's words and deeds.

Certainly, the fact that extremists like Kahane can attract any support at all should be troubling to anyone who admires the ability Israel has shown until now to maintain its institutions of democratic governance despite the circumstances in which it finds itself. That it has been able to do so, after all, is something extraordinary, even unique. Ever since its creation, Israel has been surrounded by states that, with the recent exception of Egypt, have refused to recognize, and on several occasions have tried to erase, its existence. At the same time, it has absorbed a large and expanding population of Arabs who were deeply wounded by its creation and has given them political rights – more rights, ironically, than are enjoyed by most Arabs living in Arab lands. Also at the same time, it has absorbed a still larger population of Jewish refugees who fled from Arab countries and who are very different, in their traditions and outlook, from the Western Jews who were once its majority. And, finally, it has identified itself as the unique haven for persecuted Jews – as a Jewish state – but also as a state devoted to the Western ideals of humaneness, tolerance, social justice and political equality for *all* persons, regardless of race, religion and national origin.

Whether Israel's democracy will survive will depend on its ability to continue to overcome, and successfully transform, the internal contradictions, both demographic and conceptual, that its people and institutions have faced as a result of these circumstances.

For it *is* inconsistent, in some pure and ideal sense, for a country to be a Jewish state as well as one that gives full political equality to all its citizens, including those who are not Jews. And it is inconsistent for that country to maintain a state of unblinking vigilance against efforts by the Arabs surrounding it to destroy it, and yet insist that the kinsmen of those Arabs within Israel – who believe their people to have been dispossessed by the establishment of the country, and who are increasingly nationalistic in outlook and goals – are loyal citizens of that country and can be safely entrusted to share in its governance if not in its defense. It is precisely these inconsistencies and challenges that Kahane uses to taunt his liberal critics and fellow Jews and that represent the greatest, and truest, danger to Israel's democracy – not Kahane's demagogic, religiously exclusivist and racially offensive utterances.

In the end, it will be reality, not only generous intention, that will determine whether Israel will be able to overcome these inconsistencies and challenges. Certainly, if it remains militarily capable of staving off the external Arab threat, then the power of the internal one will remain, in realistic terms, inconsequential. And if the main groups of clashing Israeli Jews sense the increasingly destructive consequences of their clashes – and the growing possibility that those clashes may, in the worst case, precipitate, for the first time in the history of the modern state, sustained incidents of Jewish civil strife – then they may be willing to pull back from the precipice of confrontation over which they could well hurl not only themselves, but also their society as a whole. There are reasons to believe that the majority of Israel's religious Jews have come to view the activities of the tiny minority among them who yearn for a theocratic state, and who seek to "hasten the coming of the Messiah" by such actions as the destruction of the Al Aqsa Mosque, to be dangerous for the country – far more dangerous, perhaps, than any realistic Arab threat. And there are reasons to believe that the majority of Oriental Jews, having finally gained positions of real political power, may recognize that the country as a whole does not have an endless capacity to withstand civil confrontation, and that such confrontation must be restrained as the dangers inherent in it become more apparent.

But what about the demographic threat that Kahane so regularly exploits with such a stinging and racial thrust? Will the Arabs ever be numerous enough to undermine Israel's Jewish identity and national existence by democratic means?

Within Israel's pre-1967 borders, most Israeli demographers believe, probably not. The high birth rate of Israeli Arabs is falling as their income and educational levels are rising, and, barring a substantial rise in Jewish emigration, will probably not result in a population that could vote out the Jewish state, at least in the foreseeable future.

The much more serious and acute demographic question relates to the West Bank and Gaza. If the territorial compromise plan favored by the Labor Party – which favors the retention of relatively unpopulated but strategically important parts of the West Bank, and the return to Jordan of the heavily populated parts – is not realized, and if the West Bank and Gaza are eventually annexed, the possibilities narrow considerably. If the Arabs within the West Bank and Gaza are granted citizenship, and choose to exercise it, Israel will very quickly become – as most Israelis, ranging from the Gush Emunim to the members of Peace Now, fear – a binational rather than a Jewish state; if the Arabs are not granted citizenship, Israel will no longer be – as most Israelis, ranging from Peace Now to some members of the Gush Emunim, also fear – a democratic state.

Thus the ironic dilemma for the Israeli democrat. If Israel retains the West Bank, it will retain not only a place that some Israelis feel is the historical heart of the Jewish homeland, but also a significant margin of strategic safety; but, in doing so, it will also retain that place's Arabs, who will rob Israel not only of its safety but also its very existence as the Jewish national home if they are granted full democratic rights and then exercise those rights to dismantle the Jewish state.

In some respects, then, Kahane is, despite his exaggerations and demagogy, right. If Israel annexes the West Bank, it cannot be both fully Jewish and fully democratic. And so at the same time as Kahane has posed a challenge to Israeli democracy by polarizing the country's various ethnic and religious communities, he has posed an even greater challenge to it by forcing it to contemplate the demographic realities that threaten to engulf and extinguish it if it fails to solve the problem of sovereignty over the West Bank – or, choosing to ignore that problem, if it extends its rare and life-giving principles, in what could amount to an act of benevolent suicide, to the territory's land and people.

Whose Homeland?

The Kahane factor deepens the essential dilemma of the West Bank, not only for Israel but for the West Bank's Arabs as well. For Israel, it reveals the vulnerability of some of its citizens to extremism under the hostile circumstances that surround them, and brings to premature but instructive immediacy the frightening alternatives that Israel could well face if it ever annexes the West Bank – either demographic engulfment, if it offers the Arabs the right to vote for the Knesset, or disintegration of its democratic principles if it does not.

For the West Bank's Arabs, the success of Kahane, limited though it is, reveals the willingness of some Israelis to compromise Israeli democracy in the service of national survival – not only those Israelis who make up Kahane's small group of ideological followers but also a much larger group who are frightened that there may be no other way than his out of their country's impasse. And, too, it raises concerns that, if an accommodation on the West Bank is not reached, Kahane's arguments may come to be more widely accepted in Israel than they are now, leaving those Arabs at ever greater risk, with the passing of each year, for the danger that serious efforts may one day be undertaken by some Israelis – to the horror of most of the rest – to dislodge them, or at least encourage them to leave, from the only place they have known as home.

118

But the essential dilemma of the West Bank – the one of simultaneous and parallel claims by Jews and Arabs to ownership, homeland and historical rights – remains even if we discount altogether Kahane and his limited influence. For those claims are present enough without him, and far more important and abiding than the twisted deepening he brings to them.

In fact, as I ended my visits to the West Bank, I found myself, in the face of that dilemma, on the edge of despair. So much of what I had heard from Arabs seemed an echo of what I had heard from Jews. So much of the passion on both sides was the same, so much of the claim, so much of the appeal to justice and history, and so much of the distrust, that the entire matter seemed impossible to resolve.

And maybe it *is* impossible to resolve. After all, the Jewish settlers really do feel their claim deeply, and really do believe that the Palestinians will never be satisfied until they have all of Israel; and many other Israelis agree with them.

And that belief is not without foundation. The PLO fosters it by repeatedly issuing resolutions that Israel must be eliminated, such as the one issued by its main constituent, *Al-Fatah*, which in 1980 declared that its aim was to "liquidate the Zionist entity politically, economically, militarily, culturally and ideologically." Moreover, the PLO's leaders and representatives have made it plain, not only at the beginning of the organization's existence but also recently, that, should they ever have the opportunity to establish an independent Palestinian state in the West Bank and Gaza, they would use it as a base from which to destroy Israel. For example, Farouk Kadoumi, the head of the PLO's political department, told *Newsweek:* "There are two phases to our return. The first phase to the 1967 lines and the second to the 1948 lines." Another PLO official, Rafik Natasha, observed: "We were not established in 1965 in order to liberate Hebron, Nablus and Gaza, for these were already liberated, but rather we were established to liberate Jaffa, Haifa, Ramla and the Negev." George Habash, head of the Popular Front for the Liberation of Palestine, told an Athens newspaper: "Yes, we will accept part of Palestine in the beginning, but under no circumstances will we agree to stop there. We will fight until we take every last corner of it." Abu Iyad, Yasser Arafat's deputy and the founder of Black September, told an interviewer: "An independent state on the West Bank and the Gaza Strip is the beginning of the final solution. That solution is to establish a democratic state in the whole of Palestine." And *Al-Talak*, a PLO organ in Syria, defined what U.S. recognition of the PLO would mean: "recognition of its rights to self-determination, beginning with an independent national state which, in the future, will demand . . . the return of Palestinian lands beyond the West Bank and the Gaza Strip – in Galilee, the coastal area, and the Negev. It [would mean] a speedy effort to regain all our rights, not just some of them."

Nor are these merely dated sentiments that have undergone maturation and revision. The Palestine National Council, established as the Palestinians' parliament-in-exile, confirmed at its meeting in Amman in November 1984 its support for pursuing the "armed struggle," its rejection of peace with Israel, and its rejection of the Camp David Accords and U.N. Security Council Resolution 242, which calls for an exchange of territory held by Israel for peace. And, at that same meeting, Abu Iyad repeated his call for the elimination of Israel: "Every one of us wants the return of Jaffa, of every centimeter of Palestinian land . . . We have said before that we want a secular, democratic state in all of Palestine. We have not gone back on that. But every stage in its time . . . The Zionists took Palestine step by step, and we must restore it step by step."

For their part, the Palestinians feel their claim no less deeply and distrust Israeli intentions no less powerfully – their distrust fed by the repeated references they hear to the Land of Israel, a land whose classical borders, they know, extend beyond the Jordan, as well as by the fact that each Arab-Israeli war has brought more territory under Israeli control. Though some Arabs recognize that there are many Israelis who would be willing to trade territory for peace, they argue that that willingness has never been translated into government policy, even after the transition, following the election of July 1984, from the Likud government, headed by Begin's successor, Yitzhak Shamir, to the national unity government initially headed by the Labor Party's more-accommodating Shimon Peres.

So *is* the West Bank dilemma impossible to resolve? Could *some* way be found to resolve the competing claims – a way that would at least partially satisfy the needs of each side, and yet be stable enough to work and last?

=========

Certainly, the most widely-sought way, at least in recent years, has involved maneuverings toward negotiations that would include Israel, Jordan and a representative body of Palestinians from the West Bank and Gaza as well as from the surrounding Arab countries. Central to these maneuverings has been the United States, the only superpower with a credible role as a mediator between Arabs and Jews. While the Soviet Union has maintained strong alliances with several of the Arab states, as well as with the PLO, it has not had relations with Israel since it broke them at the time of the 1967 Six-Day War, announcing then that it would reopen its embassy only after Israel withdrew from all occupied Arab lands. The U.S., on the other hand, has been an ally and benefactor of both Israel and, to a lesser extent, Jordan, and has also maintained important ties with other Arab states, notably Egypt and Saudi Arabia. While many Palestinians, especially those in the PLO, have considered the United States an enemy of their cause, they have recognized its potentially crucial, or at least unique, capacity to play a mediating role in the Arab-Israeli conflict, and have accepted that role to a very considerable extent, though not without strong feelings of distrust.

Israel, for its part, has viewed the PLO, since its creation in 1965, as a terrorist organization bent on its destruction, and has refused to recognize or negotiate with it. In 1975, partly in return for Israel's agreement to a partial disengagement of forces in the Sinai following its 1973 Yom Kippur War with Egypt, Henry Kissinger, then the U.S. Secretary of State, issued a written commitment to Israel restricting American dealings with the PLO, a commitment that was expanded and passed into law in October 1984 by the Congress, which specifically prohibited any American representative from recognizing or negotiating with the PLO so long as that organization "does not recognize Israel's right to exist, does not accept Security Council Resolutions 242 and 338, and does not renounce the use of terrorism."

To a great extent, Resolutions 242 and 338 have become the bedrock for all potential negotiations regarding the West Bank, as they were for the Camp David accords signed by Israel and Egypt in 1979; in addition, they have become the litmus test used to determine whether a potential negotiating partner is ready for negotiations. Resolution 242, adopted on November 22, 1967, five months after the Six-Day War, called for Israeli withdrawal "from territories occupied in the recent conflict." The Arabs have interpreted the resolution as requiring Israeli withdrawal from *all* the territories; Israel, for its part, has insisted that the words "all" or "the" were purposely excluded so as not to specify that a total withdrawal was required. And, in fact, several of the authors of that resolution, as well as the U.S. government, have agreed with the Israeli interpretation. Lord Caradon – who, as the British ambassador to the U.N. at the time, helped draft the resolution – has written that "It would have been wrong to demand that Israel return to its positions of June 4, 1967, because those positions were artificial and undesirable." And American presidents have argued similarly, Ronald Reagan noting, in connection with his introduction on September 1, 1982, of what came to be known as the Reagan Plan for a Middle East settlement, that Israel "has a right to exist behind secure and defensible borders, and it has a right to demand of its neighbors that they recognize those facts . . . In the pre-1967 borders Israel was barely 10 miles wide at its narrowest point. The bulk of Israel's population lived within artillery range of hostile Arab armies. I am not about to ask

Israel to live that way again."*

Exactly how much less than total Israel's withdrawal from the West Bank was to be, however, became a matter for debate, not only between Israel and the U.S. but also within Israel itself. The original Labor Party idea for withdrawal, the Allon Plan, called for maximal withdrawal from areas with substantial Arab population but retention of the Jordan Valley rift, a portion of the West Bank along the Dead Sea, and various border adjustments. The Likud, however, rejected any withdrawal, and, after the Israeli withdrawal from the Sinai in satisfaction of the Camp David accords, argued that that was withdrawal enough from "territories occupied in the recent conflict," and that the West Bank would never be given up. Both parties refused to consider the abandonment of East Jerusalem.

Officially, the U.S. favors, in the words of the speech announcing the Reagan Plan, "self-government by the Palestinians of the West Bank and Gaza in association with Jordan." It has rejected the idea of an independent Palestinian state – an idea favored by the PLO but probably not, ultimately, by Jordan – on the basis of a number of assumptions, most of which are widely shared by American officials: (1) Such a state would surely be governed by the PLO, either initially or eventually, no matter what arrangements are made in a peace treaty. (2) It would probably be unstable. (3) It would at some point once again express the PLO's long-held hope of liberating the rest of Palestine, even if the PLO officially abandons that hope during negotiations. (4) It would eventually attempt, through terrorism or formal military efforts, to realize that hope. (5) It might eventually try to topple the American-allied King Hussein, especially if he attempts to interfere in its affairs. (6) It might allow itself to be used by the Soviets as a base for local influence and even troops.

On February 11, 1985, after discussions with and encouragement from President Hosni Mubarak of Egypt, King Hussein

*U.N. Security Council Resolutions 242 and 338, as well as the speech introducing the Reagan Plan, are included in Appendix B.

and Yasser Arafat announced an agreement that would be the basis for a joint approach to negotiations. Included among its principles were the convening of an international peace conference; the establishment of a joint delegation of Jordanians and Palestinians; Palestinian "self-determination," a phrase that usually means the creation of a Palestinian state; and the eventual "confederation" of that state with Jordan. Although an earlier Arafat-Hussein agreement to give Jordan the right to negotiate for the Palestinians was ultimately stillborn in April 1983 because it was rejected by the PLO, this agreement did manage to garner sufficient support within the organization, at least in its general outlines, to survive initial discussions, and was then pursued aggressively by Hussein during his visit to the United States in May 1985 and backed by President Mubarak. Ironically, the PLO's support for this agreement may have been an indirect result of the failed attempt to consummate the earlier one; for it was after the earlier one was formulated – a formulation that involved a willingness to consider the 1982 Reagan Plan – that members of Arafat's *Fatah* faction in the PLO revolted against him and, in effect, formed a separate organization, centered in Damascus, that left the remaining part of the PLO that was still under Arafat's leadership more inclined to accept his decisions and agreements.

The reactions by American officials to Hussein's proposal were favorable in many respects, since they saw any movement toward negotiations as valuable. However, they objected to the fact that Arafat continued to refuse to specifically accept Resolution 242, despite Hussein's insistence that both Arafat and the PLO did. In addition, they objected to Hussein's stress on the need for an international conference under whose auspices negotiations would be held – a conference that would presumably include the Soviets – rather than on direct negotiations between Israel and a Jordanian-Palestinian delegation. Besides their belief that the Soviet Union would use such a conference for its own ends rather than the end of peace – and in fact scuttle any chance for an accommodation by encouraging maximalist demands on the part of the Arabs – Reagan administration officials recalled their own criticisms of President Jimmy Carter for having wanted, in 1977, to revive the aborted Geneva conference on the Middle East that had been sponsored by the United States and the Soviet Union in 1973.

━━━━━━━━

Israel's difficulties with Hussein's proposals were considerably more substantial. It, too, wanted only direct Arab-Israeli negotiations, and opposed any international conference; and, in addition, it feared that such a process could lead to American dealings with the PLO, and possibly even American acceptance of the principle of an independent Palestinian state.

But as profound as Israel's doubts were about the substance of the proposals, its skepticism about the possibility of a useful outcome was even more profound. And this skepticism was felt not only by the Likud members of Israel's coalition government – who opposed the very idea of territorial compromise and insisted instead on the Camp David "autonomy" approach – but almost as much by many of the coalition's Labor ministers, who were inclined to accept some kind of territorial compromise.

Most of that skepticism was centered on the roles of Arafat and the PLO. After all, the Arafat who had reached the agreement with Hussein was the same Arafat who, a month after reaching that agreement, and a month before Hussein assured the Reagan administration that Arafat was seriously hoping to achieve his goals through peaceful means rather than terrorism, sent a ship carrying 28 of his *Fatah* fighters to attack Tel Aviv – presumably the city's civilians, as similar seaborne operations had done on several occasions in previous years.

Moreover, Israelis believed that there was less reason than ever before to think that an agreement by Arafat could ever really represent an agreement by the Palestinians as a whole. While most Palestinians in the West Bank appear to support him, much of that support has become more a kind of disappointed sympathy than militant solidarity. After his long years of struggle and failure to achieve a homeland for his people, after the many opportunities to achieve such a homeland that he seemed to have in his grasp and then passed up, and after the ignominy of his expulsions – first from Beirut at the hands of Israel and then from northern Lebanon at the hands of the PLO forces that had revolted against his rule – Israelis know that many Palestinians, both in the West Bank and elsewhere, have become doubtful about his capacity to accomplish much more than his own personal survival.

For some Palestinians, in fact, it is the hard-line example set by Palestinian leaders such as Ahmed Jibril that has seemed more promising than the one set by Arafat. Jibril is the Damascus-based head of the tiny and extremist Popular Front for the Liberation of Palestine – General Command which, in 1968, split from George Habash's Popular Front for the Liberation of Palestine and, in 1983, joined the rebellion against Arafat. In May 1985, Jibril managed to defeat and humiliate Israel by forcing it to release 1,150 prisoners, many of them notorious terrorists convicted of killing numerous civilians, and to allow many of those prisoners to remain in the West Bank and Gaza as free men, in exchange for the release of three Israeli soldiers that had been captured in Lebanon. If Jibril could rub mighty Israel's nose in the mud like that, refusing repeatedly to modify his demands during the negotiations that led to the exchange – in fact, sometimes *increasing* those demands when Israel balked at them – then perhaps it was precisely such rough tactics, rather than Arafat's more compromising ones, that might in the end subdue Israel altogether and help the Palestinians gain not only a state in the West Bank but also, perhaps, the liberation, as Jibril planned, of the rest of Palestine. Besides, wasn't it just such uncompromising tactics, characterized by terrorism and the willingness to die, that had defeated and humiliated Israelis in a much more spectacular way in southern Lebanon? Wasn't it the Lebanese Shiites' readiness to blow themselves up in the service of blowing up their Israeli occupiers that had managed to do what no Palestinians, indeed, no Arabs, had ever managed to do – frighten Israeli soldiers and force them to run back home? Maybe the Shiites, in their choice of tactics, knew something that Arafat didn't know, or had forgotten; and maybe they were worthy of emulation.

But even for some of Arafat's own followers, his willingness to flirt with the idea of accepting Resolution 242 – and with it Israel's right to exist – seemed too much to swallow, especially after 18 years of PLO resolutions specifically rejecting such thoughts. In April 1985, well after Arafat's agreement was made with Hussein for a joint framework for negotiations, and just as the king was preparing to assure President Reagan that Arafat had agreed to accept Resolution 242 and was prepared to seek peace rather than wage unending war, one of Arafat's aides, Farouk Kadoumi, told a Dubai newspaper, *Al Bayan*, that 242 "cannot be recognized and anyone claiming that the PLO has recognized it is wrong." And, two weeks later, another Arafat aide, Khalil al-Wazir, also known as Abu Jihad, insisted, according to the Kuwait News Agency, that "the main option for the revolution is armed struggle," and that "political movements were never an alternative for armed struggle . . ."

And, finally, the PLO's distrust of Hussein – whose 1970 expulsion of the organization from Jordan, with a reported 7,000 to 8,000 PLO casualties, came to be known as "Black September" – remains substantial. The idea that Hussein, in joining the PLO, is really working for the Palestinians rather than himself – that he really intends to give the West Bank, once he wrests it from Israel in negotiations, to them rather than restore it to his own kingdom – seems, to some Palestinians, doubtful, even absurd. When in December 1984, Rashid Khalidi, a Palestinian academic at Columbia University, was asked about the possibility that Hussein might represent Palestinians in negotiations, he answered: "We are no more likely to let that murderer Hussein talk for us than we are Assad. Hussein uses phrases like a 'joint Palestinian-Arab delegation' or a 'joint Palestinian-Jordanian delegation.' It doesn't matter so much what you call it. The most important thing is who is the fig leaf and for whom. Would the Palestinians be serving as a fig leaf for Hussein so that he can recover the West Bank? Or would Hussein be a fig leaf for the Palestinians, so that they can pass muster in President Reagan's eyes? Assuming we do arrive at the stage of negotiations, will the Palestinians be free if the negotiations succeed, or will they just have a different master?"

But, for many Israelis, even more telling than their skepticism about the eventual success of any peace efforts that might involve Arafat or the PLO or even Hussein has been their sense that, in the end, any concrete efforts at territorial compromise would result in failure, not only because the Palestinians and Hussein would reject them, but also because so would many Israelis. "Hussein likes to live," David Levy, a high Likud official and the Housing Minister in the national unity government created in 1984, told a reporter in March 1985; "and he knows he cannot afford to give up a half, or a fourth, of Judea and Samaria. And neither will Israel share like that, not one-half, not one-fourth. We have to talk about political sharing, about autonomy for the people who live there, but not about territory." And even Ezer Weizman, a self-described Israeli "hawk for peace," has indicated that there are limits to the Israeli willingness to compromise on territory – limits that have been unacceptable, at least so far, to all Arabs, including Hussein. A former fighter pilot for the British in World War II, commander of the Israeli Air Force, and then Israeli Defense Minister under Menachem Begin, who ultimately dismissed him because of policy differences, Weizmann, like Levy a member of Israel's national unity government, has moved from hard-line leanings to accommodationist ones – a shift probably influenced by his involvement in the Camp David negotiations, during which he developed a strong friendship with Anwar Sadat. The results of that shift were evident during his service as Defense Minister, when he tried to be as lenient as possible in his reactions to Arab violence in the West Bank, provoking the ire of Jewish settlers, who complained of his refusal to crack down on Arab stone-throwers – a complaint subsequently cited by the Jewish terrorist underground during their trials as justification for taking the law into their own hands. Asked about the 1985 Hussein initiative to negotiate on the West Bank, Weizman implied that the king was fooling himself if he thought that he would be able to achieve even his, not to speak of the PLO's, demands. "I do hope King Hussein understands," Weizman observed, "that he will never have Jerusalem back."

═══════════

Yet there is an even more serious reason to believe that no Israeli government, whether a hard-line one or an accommodationist one, could ever bring itself to make near-total concession on the West Bank. For, as much opposition as such concessions would provoke among mainstream Israelis – opposition on the grounds, primarily, of security concerns – the opposition provoked by the settlers themselves, and by their supporters in Israel, would be far greater, and have consequences of such profound proportions, that they would bring the very survival of the state into question.

For, to many of the settlers, especially the members of the Gush Emunim, the West Bank is not simply territory that can be given up if something better – namely peace – is available in exchange. Even if peace *were* available in exchange – something the Gush Emunim, as well as many Israelis, have reason to doubt – such an exchange would be simply impermissible. You don't exchange your own home, especially if it was, as Rabbi Moshe Levinger and other members of the Gush Emunim believe, God-given. For it was, after all, God himself, in Numbers 33:53-54, who said: "And you shall take possession of the land and settle in it, for I have given the land to you to possess it." And it was the classical medieval commentator, Nachmanides, who taught, on the basis of this verse: "We are commanded to take possession of the land . . . we should not leave it in the hands of any other people to allow it to be waste." Nachmanides went on: "We are commanded to enter the land, to conquer its cities, and to settle our tribes there . . . for this is the commandment of conquest."

For many in the Gush Emunim, that commandment is as binding on the Jewish people today as it was in the time of Joshua. And the Six-Day War, which made the realization of that commandment possible in the heart of the ancient

homeland, was a miracle that not only saved Israel from
destruction but had also ushered in a messianic age at the end of
which personal salvation as well as national redemption would
occur. For these people, the land is not only important
historically and personally but also cosmically; it is sacred in an
ultimate and literal sense, and relinquishing it would amount to
nothing less than the profaning of a holy process, an interference
in the elaboration of God's will, and a subversion of a divine
plan begun with, and centered on, the Jews' full and final return
to their land of origin.

For the Gush Emunim members who hold this view, as well
as for other settlers for whom a withdrawal from the West Bank
would represent an abandonment of history and of national
rights, any effort on the part of an Israeli government to
dislodge them would probably result in communal violence of
substantial proportions, even civil war. When Israeli soldiers
entered Yamit in northern Sinai to dismantle that Jewish
settlement in anticipation of the return of the Sinai to Egypt,
some Yamit settlers, as well as settlers who came from the West
Bank, threatened to kill themselves, or even to fight Israeli
soldiers, rather than allow such a dismantling to occur. But
Yamit was, after all, only in the Sinai, in a peripheral part of the
ancient Land of Israel, and the threats were never carried out. In
the heart of that land, however – in the West Bank – they
probably would. Civil violence – Jews killing Jews, or Jews,
Masada-like, killing themselves – could well erupt, mirroring the
tragic circumstances of bloody strife that marked the end of
Jewish national existence in Judea two millennia ago. In the face
of such a possibility – one that, at the worst, could lead to the
dissolution of Israel itself – it seems extremely unlikely that any
Israeli government would find itself able to abandon all of the
West Bank, or perhaps even most of it. For even if negotiations
would proceed, and even if the Israeli government were to find
itself ready to make such concessions, the very possibility that
these concessions might be made could be enough to spur
protests and violence. In the end, the danger of national
self-destruction, or at least severe damage, would seem so great

that any Israeli government would probably find the danger of continuing occupation less frightening and, therefore, more acceptable.

And even if, as part of an accommodation that transfers the West Bank to full Arab rule, the settlements and the settlers were granted the right to stay, the prospects of violence would probably be no less substantial. To begin with, the very idea of Jewish settlements continuing to exist in peace under Arab control seems unlikely in the extreme. Such an idea – held by, among other Israelis, Abba Eban – flies in the face of the history and reality of the Arab-Israeli conflict, as well as the passions that that conflict has engendered. To Eban, such settlements would be analogous to the settlements of Arabs within pre-1967 Israel. But those Arabs lived in those settlements before Israel was founded, while the Jewish settlers moved into the West Bank settlements only after that area was conquered in a war. While Israel, for its part, insisted, both before the state was established and after, that the Arabs in Israel were welcome to live there and eligible for citizenship, all Arabs have declared the West Bank Jewish settlements unacceptable, including the West Bank Arabs I interviewed, such as Mustafa Natshe and Bassam Shaka'a. If the West Bank were, in fact, to be given over to Arab administration – as a self-governing area in association with Jordan, as part of Jordan, or as an independent Palestinian state – the very great likelihood is that Jewish settlers there, even if they accepted local citizenship, would become the targets for continuing attacks and massacres, provoking protective responses from Israel, including repeated incursions, and perhaps even, ultimately, re-occupation. Besides, it seems overwhelmingly likely that the settlers would view the option of continuing to live in the West Bank under full Arab rule as unacceptable, and a justification for violent protests, even if they could be somehow certain that they would be left to live in peace in the heart of the Land of Israel. For their goals are, after all, far less personal than they are national; and so the greatest disaster they fear is not the dismantling of the settlements but the withdrawal of Israeli control from the heart of the Land of

Israel. The withdrawal of that control would almost surely result in violence; and it would be the prospect of that violence that would probably paralyze the hand of any Israeli leader otherwise ready to give away what the settlers, as well as other Israelis, would see as too much.

So the chances for reaching a settlement through negotiations that involve the PLO, particularly under international auspices, seem small indeed. The PLO is unlikely to be able to survive, even in its currently fractured form, if it formally and publicly abandons, even for tactical reasons alone, its long-held insistence on nothing short of the creation of an independent Palestinian state. And Israel is unlikely, for its own internal reasons, to agree to a settlement that would be even half-acceptable to the PLO, or even to Hussein.

Does this mean that no accommodation on the West Bank is possible?

It doesn't mean that, but it probably does mean that other routes will have to be found if such an accommodation is to be achieved – and that the nature of that accommodation, if it *is* achieved, will probably be different from the one generally envisioned until now.

The route that is most likely to achieve at least some success in reaching a West Bank accommodation would probably involve negotiations, at least initially, between Israel and the West Bank Palestinians themselves. And to understand why, it is important to recognize that the West Bank Palestinians constitute, by now, a group within the greater Palestinian fold that is distinctive from other Palestinians, not only geographically but also historically.

For the Palestinian population can be considered to have been made up, since 1967, of two communities seeking a solution to their unresolved national condition. One of these communities consists of Palestinians who live in the West Bank and Gaza, which is to say in Palestine itself, or, to be precise, in the part of the original Palestine Mandate that came to be called Palestine after Transjordan was severed from it; they number some 2 million.*

Until now, the Palestinian community outside of Palestine has been the one that has been active politically and militarily. That community has sustained the PLO, established itself as an international force, and mobilized an array of allies for the purpose of battling Israel and liberating its homeland. By contrast, the Palestinian community in the West Bank and Gaza, dominated by Israel, has been politically subdued; but it has generally – and, until recent years, strongly – given the other community its moral support and blessing, as well as its proxy for action, by recognizing the PLO as its representative.

It is ironic, however, that, in doing so – in backing an organization and a community whose goals are probably not attainable – the Palestinians living in the West Bank have made it impossible for themselves to pursue goals that would benefit them, and perhaps also their brethren outside the West Bank, considerably, and that are, in any case, more attainable.

For, in important ways, the goals of the two Palestinian communities, though they overlap, are different; and the difference has to do with the different geographic histories the two communities have experienced.

The Palestinians living outside of Palestine are, in the main, the Palestinians or the descendants of the Palestinians, originally numbering 500,000 to 700,000, who lost their homes and property when Israel was first created. It is they who became, and in large measure remained and were encouraged to remain, refugees in the surrounding Arab states. And it is they, therefore, who for nearly four decades have been nurtured on the dream of returning to their homes and property in what is now Israel, and who created the PLO to engineer that return, retake their original homes and property, and achieve a state in all of Palestine, including the part in which they or their parents

*For the derivation of these figures, see Appendix A.

once lived. For that Palestinian community the goal remains essentially the same; it has never been changed, at least not formally. To change it would be to abandon the dream that fired the hopes and imaginations of the community and that served as the basis for all of its political, social and cultural organizations; to abandon it would be to abandon the cohesion and life of the community itself. It is for this reason that every attempt by Arafat or other Palestinians in the PLO to consider an accommodation has caused cataclysms within the organization. For accommodation means, at the very least, a recognition of Israel within its pre-1967 borders, which involves a recognition that that part of Palestine – the part from which they or their parents or grandparents came – is no longer available for them as a homeland. Nor is it easy even to utter, for tactical, negotiating reasons, words that would feign such a stance; for it is in part precisely to make sure that no Palestinian would ever utter such words, and in the end give up the dream of liberation and return, that the Palestinian National Charter, as well as resolution after resolution and statement after statement, have repeated the insistence that it is the liberation of and return to *all* of Palestine, not just the West Bank, that is the goal of Palestinian nationalism. It is for this reason, more than any other, that the hard-line faction of the PLO split itself away from Arafat's leadership in 1983, when he was willing to consider the Reagan Plan that would have yielded something less than a Palestinian state and that would have required the formal recognition that part of Palestine was irretrievably lost; and it is for this reason, more than any other, that it has been so hard for Arafat, despite the tactical advantages that would be gained from doing so, to utter an acceptance of Resolution 242, which would imply such a recognition.

The great bulk of the Palestinians in the West Bank, on the other hand, were born there and are the children of Palestinians who were born there; neither they nor their parents ever lived in what is now Israel. Though some – such as the former acting mayor of Hebron, Mustafa Natshe – owned property in the area of Palestine that became Israel, most did not. For these

Palestinians, an accommodation with Israel that resulted in a territory that was in some fashion independent or self-governed – either a full-fledged, if perhaps truncated, West Bank Palestinian state that includes Gaza, or a West Bank-Gaza entity federated with Jordan – would provide, finally, control over their own land, something they had not been allowed by Arabs from 1948 to 1967, and have not been allowed by Israel since then. But such an accommodation, if it could be reached, would inevitably require the abandonment of all claims to political rights on the part of Palestine that is now Israel – that is, Israel within its pre-1967 borders; and such an abandonment would represent a betrayal of the interests of the other Palestinian community, the one outside Palestine. To be sure, not a complete betrayal: property rights could be recognized through the arrangement of compensation for property lost, and even through permission given to refugees to live in Israel, as part of an overall settlement. But political rights would be abandoned – an abandonment that would betray the dream of the return.

But that dream in its fullness is, under the present and foreseeable political and military circumstances, simply un-attainable, whereas the modified dream, the establishment of an independent or federated or autonomous Palestinian West Bank, is, at least in some form, still attainable, though, given the continuing enlargement of Jewish settlements, not for long. It would therefore seem to be in the interests of the West Bank Palestinians to attempt to realize that modified dream as soon as possible; and insofar as that realization would yield at least some benefits to the refugees in the Palestinian community outside Palestine – perhaps compensation for lost property as well as the right to live at least in the West Bank and possibly near their original homes in Israel – it would be in the interest of that community as well.

Is it likely that the West Bank Palestinians would be willing, after all these years of resistance to the idea, to make that attempt – to seize the moment of opportunity that may now be available to them, to depart from the PLO line, and to declare themselves ready to recognize and negotiate with Israel? It may not be likely, but it is, as a result of the split in the PLO, just possible. Because of that split, the requirement that West Bank Palestinians maintain unity behind the PLO position has lost much of its logic, given the lack of unity within the PLO itself; and, as the split has grown, so have the possibilities for expressing independent West Bank Palestinian views.

An early expression of such views took place in December 1983, some nine months after the split began, when a bomb planted in a Jerusalem bus killed six Israelis and wounded forty-five. Immediately after the blast, both factions of the PLO – Arafat's, which was still besieged in Tripoli, in northern Lebanon, and his rival Abu Musa's, which was doing the besieging – claimed responsibility for it. Within a few days, five prominent West Bank Palestinian leaders issued a statement deploring the act. One of those leaders was Mustafa Natshe, the dismissed acting mayor of Hebron; until then, Natshe would never have questioned a PLO-endorsed act, at least not publicly. Another signer of the statement was Paul Ajlouny, the publisher of *Al-Fajr*, the pro-PLO East Jerusalem Palestinian newspaper.

If such West Bank Palestinians would be willing not only to disagree with the PLO publicly but also to offer to negotiate with Israel in their own names as well as in the name of the Palestinians as a whole, then at least some progress might be made toward an Arab-Israeli accommodation. The first step in that process would probably have to be a declaration on the part of those Palestinians that they were willing to accept Israel within its pre-1967 borders, and that they recognized that some of those borders would have to be revised so as to satisfy Israel's legitimate security concerns.

If West Bank Palestinian leaders were to take that step, this could well provoke a very substantial upheaval within Israeli society. Those Israelis who have favored the retention of the West Bank on the grounds of security would suddenly have reason to feel a little less insecure. Not that their insecurity would disappear altogether. Many would continue to worry that the West Bank Palestinians' recognition of Israel was only, as Karim told me when I interviewed him, a negotiating tactic to achieve a West Bank state as a springboard for the liberation of the rest of Palestine. But such recognition would, after all, constitute the most significant change in the Palestinian position in decades, and would be seen by large numbers of Israelis as significant enough to make the risks posed by an accommodation on the West Bank worthwhile.

The details of the agreement that might be forged in negotiations between West Bank Palestinians willing to speak for themselves and an Israeli government willing to risk its future security, not to speak of its internal cohesion, are hard to predict. But it might well be possible to construct an arrangement in which the West Bank Palestinians, together with the Palestinians living in Gaza, would have civil and perhaps also political independence; in which the right of Palestinian refugees from the surrounding states to live in the West Bank and Gaza could be guaranteed; and in which compensation to Palestinians who lost property in Israel in 1948 could be made, along with compensation to Jews who lost property in Arab countries when they fled or were expelled at around the same time.

What about the question of territory and Jewish settlement? That question would be a very difficult one indeed, and would have to be solved if the rest of the solution is to be achieved. Clearly, significant border changes would have to be made to render the populous coastal plain of Israel, its ten-mile-wide vulnerable throat, less vulnerable. In addition, an Israeli military presence, at least for a limited period, would have to be maintained in the Jordan Valley rift. And it seems inconceivable that Israel would agree to give up sovereignty over any part of Jerusalem.

In order to solve the problem of the existing Jewish settlements a number of solutions have been offered that would divide up the West Bank either administratively or geographically so as to keep the two populations apart and in control of their own destinies. The administrative solutions – such as a "condominium" of the West Bank, with ownership shared by Israel and Jordan, and with the two populations, Arab and Jewish, voting in the two separate states – is logical on paper but may be utterly unworkable, given the long-held enmities that would no doubt interfere with, and probably subvert, any enterprise that requires sharing and daily cooperation.

The geographic solutions that have been offered and that are still possible would involve a more painful loss for the Arabs, but might be more successful. One Israeli, Clinton Bailey, who teaches at Tel Aviv University, has argued that Labor's old Allon Plan, which envisaged relatively small border changes, is, given the proliferation of Jewish settlements since the plan was proposed just after the Six-Day War, no longer possible, and has outlined a plan himself that, he believes, is.

Bailey's plan would take into account the existence of the Jewish settlements and their committed residents, as well as the existence of the West Bank's overwhelming Arab majority, by dividing the territory into Arab areas that would be under Arab rule and Jewish ones that would be made part of Israel. The Arab areas, for their part, would consist of six geographic pockets, or enclaves, containing the vast majority of the Arab population but only a minority of the Jewish settlements. These enclaves, comprising almost half of the West Bank and the great bulk of its arable land – and located chiefly in the western, hilly part of the West Bank, which is the traditional site of habitation, rather than in the eastern, desert part, along the Jordan River and the Dead Sea – would be divided from each other by strips of Jewish settlement, which would become part of Israel. New roads would be built to accommodate transportation among the Jewish settlements and between them and the territory of pre-1967 Israel, and arrangements would be made to allow for easy road communication between one Arab enclave and another, within which no Jewish settlements or land acquisition would be permitted. The Arab enclaves themselves, as Bailey envisions them, could be ruled by Jordan, from which they would be physically separated by a strip of Israeli-annexed land along the Jordan River and the shore of the Dead Sea; though such a disembodied arrangement is unusual, Bailey believes that it could be made to work in much the same way that the Federal Republic of Germany's rule over a geographically separate and distant West Berlin has been made to work. Finally, Jordanian rule would consist primarily of security arrangements, with the Arab enclaves otherwise functioning autonomously in their civil and political administration.

What of the Jewish settlements in Bailey's plan? The great majority of them would be located in the strips of Israeli territory between the Arab enclaves or in the Jordan Valley, with only 20 or so existing settlements, most of them only temporary and very small, remaining in the enclaves and having to e dismantled. Wouldn't even such a limited dismantling – and particularly an abandonment by Israel of the Arab enclaves – provoke the ire and even violence of the settlers? Bailey seems to believe that, overall, the settlers could be persuaded to accept such an accommodation in the light of the fact that it would guarantee Israeli sovereignty, and Jewish settlement, in much of Judea and Samaria, and if they could be shown that the abandonment of the rest would be worthwhile, even in religious terms, on the grounds that it purchases peace and national survival. Whether this geographic solution would prove, in practical terms, more workable than an administrative one, and whether Palestinians or Jordanians would view it as nothing better than a system of South African black homelands, is hard to say; but there is at least a chance that it would be workable in human terms, and may be the only kind of solution of a territorial sort that is still possible in political terms.

Clearly, no solution would be simple, or satisfy the full aspirations of either side. In fact, the very details of any possible solution, when they are actually spelled out, tend to repel both sides by their specificity: the compromises inevitably seem blasphemous, or humiliating, or dangerous, or enraging. Still, it is in the interests of both sides to begin to reach some kind of an accommodation, and to do so quickly; and, for different reasons, both sides may be more ready than they have been to find some kind of accommodation.

For the Israelis, the nightmarish choice between demographic engulfment or democratic dissolution may well become one they will really have to face if such an accommodation is not reached. In addition, the war in Lebanon, with its 650 dead, has rendered Israel weary, and its economic difficulties have made it wearier still. And, too, internal friction within Israel's own diverse Jewish communities – communities that differ from each other in degree of religious observance or place of origin – has worsened, provoking in some Israelis deep concern, even alarm, about the country's social cohesiveness, and inclining them more than ever to seek some kind of accommodation on the until-now intractable problems that beset it from the outside.

For the West Bank Palestinians, the specter of a West Bank with a population of 100,000 Jewish settlers, or even 200,000, is no less a nightmare, and should be no less a spur to achieve *some* kind of accommodation, to get *some* piece of territory for themselves, before there is no territory left to get, or no way at all, even an unsatisfactory way, in which it could be divided up. The worst nightmare of all for these Palestinians, perhaps, is the prospect that the present opportunity for peace, as inadequate as it now seems for them, and as unlikely as it is to yield a satisfactory solution, will someday be remembered as one that was rejected but that should have been seized, much as the numerous opportunities during the past four decades – from the U.N. partition plan of 1947 to the offer by Israel just after the Six-Day War to return all or nearly all of the West Bank – were rejected rather than seized in the hope that *all* of Palestine would be liberated, and were then regretted as it came to be realized that the march of time, as well as the march of events, made that hope ever less possible, and the rejected opportunities ever more golden.

Finally, an early accommodation on the West Bank would be advantageous to Jordan and in particular to King Hussein. For, if the Palestinians do indeed lose the chance for even a part of the West Bank, or for a sharing of it, then they could well begin to direct their national aspirations elsewhere. And the most logical place to which those aspirations could be directed would be Jordan. After all, some 60% of Jordan's population is made up of Palestinians, and the Hashemites who have ruled the country – namely Hussein and his grandfather Abdullah – are themselves newcomers to the area, having entered it from the Arabian peninsula only a few decades ago. While the United States would see a takeover of Jordan by Palestinians as damaging to its interests, given Hussein's general friendship with America, there may be little it could do if the Palestinians of Jordan, Syria and Lebanon, through the PLO and perhaps with Syria's help, manage to topple the king, as some of them tried to do in 1970, and establish, finally, a Palestinian state. It may be such a prospect that, more than any other, has motivated Hussein to find an accommodation for the Palestinians in the West Bank – and that might motivate him enough in the future to accept, and encourage, a solution that, until now, neither he nor the Palestinians have been willing even to entertain.

Even though it seems that an initiative from the West Bank Palestinians would be more likely to lead to an accommodation than would negotiations that include the PLO, there is of course no certainty that such an overture will come, or, if it did, that it would be welcomed or even permitted by a suspicious and disunited Israel and by a population of Jewish settlers who would see any accommodation as endangering their own attachment to, and vision of, the land. But, if no such overture comes, and if the traditionally-used route toward accommodation – the one that includes the PLO, Jordan and international mediation – proves to be, ultimately, a failure, then the West Bank will continue to be one of the many places in the world in which the dreams of one group are enveloped by the fears of another, and in which injustice is mingled with justice in ways that are impossible to disentangle. We rarely pay attention to other such areas, because it is easy not to: the 20 million Kurds, the world has decided, are forgettable, and so, unfortunately for them, is their struggle for an independent Kurdish state. But the Israelis and the Palestinians are not forgettable, the alliances that rotate about them are powerful, and the competing claims stare us in the face with the threat of ultimate horror.

In the short run, the best chance for an accommodation, as tenuous and frayed a chance as it is, rests in the hands of the Palestinians in the West Bank. Their choice will affect not only them and their children but also the dreams and the future of all Arabs, all Jews, and perhaps all mankind.

Appendix A
The Problem of
Palestinian Population Figures

The population figures for the Palestinian Arabs living in various countries vary widely depending on the source and the interests served by those figures. Nearly all figures are disputed. It seems probable that there are about 700,000 Palestinian Arabs within pre-1967 Israel itself. They have been counted by Israel together with the Jewish population of Israel, and are Israeli citizens. The figures for the remaining Palestinians are much less certain.

In the West Bank, the likely range appears to be 700,000 to 750,000 (the U.S. State Department's estimate is the latter; the PLO's is 815,000), and in Gaza, 400,000 to 500,000 (the U.S. State Department's estimate is again the latter; the PLO's is 476,700). Thus 1.3 million seems to be a reasonable figure for the Palestinians living in the occupied territories, with 1.4 million the probable upper limit. While most of the Palestinians in the West Bank were born there, the majority of the Palestinians in Gaza – perhaps 300,000 – are persons, or the children or grandchildren of persons, who in 1948 fled from the part of Palestine that became Israel.

The estimates for the Palestinian population in the rest of the Middle East and in North Africa are even less certain than the ones for the Israeli-occupied territories. In part this is because there are no censuses of the populations as a whole in most of those countries, or because in those cases in which there are censuses – such as, apparently, Syria – complete figures are not made public. Generally, the lack of a census appears to be a result of the wish on the part of a government to not reveal its true total population or the true percentage of the total population that is made up of one or another segment of that population. For example, an accurate census would probably reveal that Saudi Arabia's population is much smaller than the one it claims, with an alarmingly high percentage of that population being made up of foreigners. Kuwait, similarly, has a disturbingly high percentage of non-citizens in its midst – probably at

143

least 50 percent – and probably prefers not to publicize that circumstance.

Another reason for the varying figures for Palestinians are the interests served by those figures. For Israel, it would be better if there were fewer who were displaced by its creation in 1948, or who are the offspring of those who were displaced; hence its figures are probably low. For the PLO, it would clearly be better if more Palestinians could be said to belong in those categories; the greater the figures, the greater the injustice and the more pressing the claim. In addition, various agencies, particularly the United Nations Relief and Works Agency, provide financial aid to persons they identify as Palestinian refugees; and there are said to be many Palestinians on the rolls of this agency who are by all ordinary definitions fully resettled but who continue to obtain aid nevertheless – as do others who, it has been reported, died long ago. Unfortunately, UNRWA's figures influence the figures issued by other sources.

Despite the great uncertainty regarding Palestinian population figures outside of Israel and the occupied territories of the West Bank and Gaza, some guesses are worth making. Of Jordan's approximately 2 million population (the estimates range from 1.8 million to 2.4 million), about 60 to 65 percent, or some 1.2 million, are of western Palestinian origin (the State Department estimates 1 million, the PLO 1.18 million); all have, or have the right to have, Jordanian citizenship, as do all West Bank Palestinians. Of the western Palestinians in Jordan, the great majority are integrated fully into Jordanian society; perhaps not more than 300,000, probably fewer, can be said to be refugees.

The estimates of Palestinians in Lebanon range from 300,000 (Israel's) to 650,000 (the PLO's); the Lebanse Christians claim there are about 500,000 Palestinians in Lebanon, the Lebanese government says the figure is 600,000, and the State Department cites 400,000. In Syria, the State Department says there are 250,000; the PLO lists 215,000.

The numbers of Palestinians in other countries in the Middle East and North Africa are as follows, with figures from the State Department (most of them dating from October 1982) cited first, and with the most recent figures from the PLO cited second: Kuwait (270,000-320,000; 278,800); Saudi Arabia (120,000; 127,000); Iraq (70,000-120,000; 20,000); Egypt (50,000-60,000; 48,500); United Arab Emirates (40,000; 34,700); Qatar (16,000-20,000; 22,500); Libya (10,000-15,000; 23,000); Oman (500; 48,200, with staff of the Washington, D.C., Palestine Information Office puzzled by the discrepancy); Tunisia, as of January 1984, after the arrival of Arafat's loyalists from Tripoli (1,500-3,000; no PLO estimate); Algeria (5,000-10,000; no PLO estimate); North Yemen (1,000-2,000; no PLO estimate); South Yemen, after the arrival of Arafat's loyalists (1,200; no PLO estimate); Sudan (up to 600; no PLO estimate); Morocco (250; no PLO estimate).

Altogether, then, the total number of Palestinians living in the Middle East and North Africa outside of Israel and the occupied territories of the West

Bank and Gaza is roughly 2.4 million; and if the number of those who have
been integrated into the Jordanian population is subtracted, then the figure is
about 1.5 million. If yet another group of Palestinians is subtracted from this
figure – those who have been integrated into the societies of Middle East and
North African countries other than Jordan – the figure would probably be
about 1 to 1.3 million. This range – 1 to 1.3 million – is probably the one that
should be used as the estimate for the number of Palestinians outside of the
occupied territories whose national condition truly remains unresolved.
Nevertheless, since Palestinian spokesmen generally maintain that all
Palestinians, no matter how integrated they may be into the societies, cultures,
and economies of one country or another, are in those countries as refugees,
and are waiting to return to the homes from which they or their parents or
grandparents fled, it is not this figure of 1 to 1.3 million but rather the figure of
2 million that is used in this book.

Appendix B
Documents

The Balfour Declaration*

Foreign Office
November 2nd, 1917.

Dear Lord Rothschild,

I have much pleasure in conveying to you, on behalf of His Majesty's Government, the following declaration of sympathy with Jewish Zionist aspirations which has been submitted to, and approved by, the Cabinet.

"His Majesty's Government view with favour the establishment in Palestine of a national home for the Jewish people, and will use their best endeavours to facilitate the achievement of this object, it being clearly understood that nothing shall be done which may prejudice the civil and religious rights of existing non-Jewish communities in Palestine, or the rights and political status enjoyed by Jews in any other country."

I should be grateful if you would bring this declaration to the knowledge of the Zionist Federation.

Yours sincerely,
ARTHUR JAMES BALFOUR.

*Letter sent by Arthur James Balfour, the British Foreign Secretary, to Baron Lionel Walter Rothschild, president of the British Zionist Federation.

United Nations Security Council Resolution 242
(November 22, 1967)

THE SECURITY COUNCIL,

Expressing its continuing concern with the grave situation in the Middle East,

Emphasizing the inadmissibility of the acquisition of territory by war and the need to work for a just and lasting peace in which every state in the area can live in security.

Emphasizing further that all member states in their acceptance of the Charter of the United Nations have undertaken a commitment to act in accordance with Article 2 of the Charter,

1. *Affirms* that the fulfillment of Charter principles requires the establishment of a just and lasting peace in the Middle East which should include the application of both the following principles:

(i) Withdrawal of Israeli armed forces from territories of recent conflict;

(ii) Termination of all claims or states of belligerency and respect for and acknowledgment of the sovereignty, territorial integrity and political independence of every state in the area and their right to live in peace within secure and recognized boundaries free from threats or acts of force;

2. *Affirms further* the necessity

(a) For guaranteeing freedom of navigation through international waterways in the area;

(b) For achieving a just settlement of the refugee problem;

(c) For guaranteeing the territorial inviolability and political independence of every state in the area, through measures including the establishment of demilitarized zones;

3. *Requests* the Secretary General to designate a special representative to proceed to the Middle East to establish and maintain contacts with the states concerned in order to promote agreement and assist efforts to achieve a peaceful and accepted settlement in accordance with the provisions and principles in this resolution.

4. *Requests* the Secretary General to report to the Security Council on the progress of the efforts of the special representative as soon as possible.

United Nations Security Council Resolution 338
(October 22, 1973)

THE SECURITY COUNCIL

1. Calls upon all parties to the present fighting to cease all firing and terminate all military activity immediately, no later than 12 hours after the moment of the adoption of this decision, in the positions they now occupy;

2. Calls upon the parties concerned to start immediately after the cease-fire the implementation of Security Council Resolution 242, (1967) in all of its parts;

3. Decides that immediately and concurrently with the cease-fire, negotiations start between the parties concerned under appropriate auspices aimed at establishing a just and durable peace in the Middle East.

The Palestinian National Charter*

1. Palestine is the homeland of the Arab Palestinian people; it is an indivisible part of the Arab homeland, and the Palestinian people are an integral part of the Arab nation.

2. Palestine, with the boundaries it had during the British Mandate, is an indivisible territorial unit.

3. The Palestinian Arab people possess the legal right to their homeland and have the right to determine their destiny after achieving the liberation of their country in accordance with their wishes and entirely of their own accord and will.

4. The Palestinian identity is a genuine, essential, and inherent characteristic; it is transmitted from parents to children. The Zionist occupation and the dispersal of the Palestinian Arab people, through the disasters which befell them, do not make them lose their Palestinian identity and their membership in the Palestinian community, nor do they negate them.

5. The Palestinians are those Arab nationals who, until 1947, normally resided in Palestine regardless of whether they were evicted from it or have stayed there. Anyone born, after that date, of a Palestinian father, whether inside Palestine or outside it – is also a Palestinian.

6. The Jews who had normally resided in Palestine until the beginning of the Zionist invasion will be considered Palestinians.

7. That there is a Palestinian community and that it has material, spiritual, and historical connection with Palestine are indisputable facts. It is a national duty to bring up individual Palestinians in an Arab revolutionary manner. All means of information and education must be adopted in order to acquaint the Palestinian with his country in the most profound manner, both spiritual and material, that is possible. He must be prepared for the armed struggle and ready to sacrifice his wealth and his life in order to win back his homeland and bring about its liberation.

8. The phase in their history, through which the Palestinian people are now living, is that of national struggle for the liberation of Palestine. Thus the conflicts among the Palestinian national forces are secondary, and should be ended for the sake of the basic conflict that exists between the forces of Zionism and of imperialism on the one hand, and the Palestinian Arab people on the other. On this basis the Palestinian masses, regardless of whether they are residing in the national homeland or in diaspora, constitute – both their organizations and the individuals – one national front working for the retrieval of Palestine and its liberation through armed struggle.

9. Armed struggle is the only way to liberate Palestine. Thus it is the overall strategy, not merely a tactical phase. The Palestinian Arab people assert their

*Adopted by the National Congress of the Palestine Liberation Organization in Cairo, July 1968.

absolute determination and firm resolution to continue their armed struggle and to work for an armed popular revolution for the liberation of their country and their return to it. They also assert their right to normal life in Palestine and to exercise their right to self-determination and sovereignty over it.

10. Commando action constitutes the nucleus of the Palestinian popular liberation war. This requires its escalation, comprehensiveness, and the mobilization of all the Palestinian popular and educational efforts and their organization and involvement in the armed Palestinian revolution. It also requires the achieving of unity for the national struggle among the different groupings of the Palestinian people, and between the Palestinian people and the Arab masses, so as to secure the continuation of the revolution, its escalation, and victory.

11. The Palestinians will have three mottoes: national unity, national mobilization, and liberation.

12. The Palestinian people believe in Arab unity. In order to contribute their share toward the attainment of that objective, however they must, at the present stage of their struggle, safeguard their Palestinian identity and develop their consciousness of that identity, and oppose any plan that may dissolve or impair it.

13. Arab unity and the liberation of Palestine are two complementary objectives, the attainment of either of which facilitates the attainment of the other. Thus, Arab unity leads to the liberation of Palestine, the liberation of Palestine leads to Arab unity; and work toward the realization of one objective proceeds side by side with work toward the realization of the other.

14. The destiny of the Arab nation, and indeed Arab existence itself, depend upon the destiny of the Palestine cause. From this interdependence spring the Arab nation's pursuit of, and striving for, the liberation of Palestine. The people of Palestine play the role of the vanguard in the realization of this sacred national goal.

15. The liberation of Palestine, from an Arab viewpoint, is a national duty and it attempts to repel the Zionist and imperialist aggression against the Arab homeland, and aims at the elimination of Zionism in Palestine. Absolute responsibility for this falls upon the Arab nation – peoples and governments – with the Arab people of Palestine in the vanguard. Accordingly, the Arab nation must mobilize all its military, human, moral, and spiritual capabilities to participate actively with the Palestinian people in the liberation of Palestine. It must, particularly in the phase of the armed Palestinian revolution, offer and furnish the Palestinian people with all possible help, and material and human support, and make available to them the means and opportunities that will enable them to continue to carry out their leading role in the armed revolution, until they liberate their homeland.

16. The liberation of Palestine, from a spiritual point of view, will provide the Holy Land with an atmosphere of safety and tranquility, which in turn will safeguard the country's religious sanctuaries and guarantee freedom of

worship and of visit to all, without discrimination of race, color, language, or religion. Accordingly, the people of Palestine look to all spiritual forces in the world for support.

17. The liberation of Palestine, from a human point of view, will restore to the Palestinian individual his dignity, pride, and freedom. Accordingly the Palestinian Arab people look forward to the support of all those who believe in the dignity of man and his freedom in the world.

18. The liberation of Palestine, from an international point of view, is a defensive action necessitated by the demands of self-defense. Accordingly, the Palestine people, desirous as they are of the friendship of all people, look to freedom-loving and peace-loving states for support in order to restore their legitimate rights in Palestine, to re-establish peace and security in the country, and to enable its people to exercise national sovereignty and freedom.

19. The partition of Palestine in 1947 and the establishment of the state of Israel are entirely illegal, regardless of the passage of time, because they were contrary to the will of the Palestinian people and to their natural right in their homeland, and inconsistent with the principles embodied in the Charter of the United Nations, particularly the right to self-determination.

20. The Balfour Declaration, the Mandate for Palestine, and everything that has been based upon them, are deemed null and void. Claims of historical or religious ties of Jews with Palestine are incompatible with the facts of history and the true conception of what constitutes statehood. Judaism, being a religion, is not an independent nationality. Nor do Jews constitute a single nation with an identity of its own; they are citizens of the states to which they belong.

21. The Arab Palestinian people, expressing themselves by the armed Palestinian revolution, reject all solutions which are substitutes for the total liberation of Palestine and reject all proposals aiming at the liquidation of the Palestinian problem, or its internationalization.

22. Zionism is a political movement organically associated with international imperialism and antagonistic to all action for liberation and to progressive movements in the world. It is racist and fanatic in its nature, aggressive, expansionist, and colonial in its aims, and fascist in its methods. Israel is the instrument of the Zionist movement, and a geographical base for world imperialism placed strategically in the midst of the Arab homeland to combat the hopes of the Arab nation for liberation, unity, and progress. Israel is a constant source of threat *vis-à-vis* peace in the Middle East and the whole world. Since the liberation of Palestine will destroy the Zionist and imperialist presence and will contribute to the establishment of peace in the Middle East, the Palestinian people look for the support of all the progressive and peaceful forces and urge them all, irrespective of their affiliations and beliefs, to offer the Palestinian people all aid and support in their just struggle for the liberation of their homeland.

23. The demands of security and peace, as well as the demands of right and

justice, require all states to consider Zionism an illegitimate movement, to outlaw its existence, and to ban its operations, in order that friendly relations among peoples may be preserved, and the loyalty of citizens to their respective homelands safeguarded.

24. The Palestinian people believe in the principles of justice, freedom, sovereignty, self-determination, human dignity, and in the right of all peoples to exercise them.

25. For the realization of the goals of this Charter and its principles, the Palestine Liberation Organization will perform its role in the liberation of Palestine in accordance with the constitution of this Organization.

26. The Palestine Liberation Organization, representative of the Palestinian revolutionary forces, is responsible for the Palestinian Arab people's movement in its struggle – to retrieve its homeland, liberate and return to it and exercise the right to self-determination in it – in all military, political, and financial fields and also for whatever may be required by the Palestine case on the inter-Arab and international levels.

27. The Palestine Liberation Organization shall cooperate with all Arab states, each according to its potentialities; and will adopt a neutral policy among them in the light of the requirements of the war of liberation; and on this basis it shall not interfere in the internal affairs of any Arab state.

28. The Palestinian Arab people assert the genuineness and independence of their national revolution and reject all forms of intervention, trusteeship, and subordination.

29. The Palestinian people possess the fundamental and genuine legal right to liberate and retrieve their homeland. The Palestinian people determine their attitude toward all states and forces on the basis of the stands they adopt vis-à-vis the Palestinian case and the extent of the support they offer to the Palestinian revolution to fulfill the aims of the Palestinian people.

30. Fighters and carriers of arms in the war of liberation are the nucleus of the popular army which will be the protective force for the gains of the Palestinian Arab people.

31. The Organization shall have a flag, an oath of allegiance, and an anthem. All this shall be decided upon in accordance with a special regulation.

32. Regulations, which shall be known as the Constitution of the Palestine Liberation Organization, shall be annexed to this Charter. It shall lay down the manner in which the Organization, and its organs and institutions, shall be constituted; the respective competence of each; and the requirements of its obligations under the Charter.

33. This Charter shall not be amended save by [vote of] a majority of two-thirds of the total membership of the National Congress of the Palestine Liberation Organization [taken] at a special session convened for that purpose.

Resolutions of the Palestine National Council
(Cairo, June 1974)

1. The PLO reaffirms its previous attitude concerning Security Council

Resolution 242 which obliterates the patriotic and national rights of our people and treats our national cause as a refugee problem. It therefore refuses categorically any negotiations on the basis of this Resolution at any level of inter-Arab or international negotiation including the Geneva Conference.

2. The PLO will struggle by all possible means and foremost by means of armed struggle for the liberation of the Palestinian lands and the setting up of a patriotic, independent fighting peoples' regime in every part of the Palestine territory which will be liberated. It affirms that this will only be accomplished through major changes in the balance of forces to the advantage of our people and their struggle.

3. The PLO will struggle against any proposal to set up a Palestine entity at the price of recognition, peace and secure boundaries, giving up the historic right and depriving our people of its right to return and to self-determination on its national soil.

4. The PLO will consider any step toward liberation which is accomplished as a stage in the pursuit of its strategy for the establishment of a democratic Palestinian state, as laid down in the decisions of previous National Council meetings.

5. The PLO will struggle together with patriotic Jordanian forces for the creation of a Jordanian-Palestinian patriotic front, the object of which will be the establishment of a patriotic, democratic regime in Jordan which will make common cause with the Palestinian entity which will arise as a result of struggle and conflict.

6. The PLO will struggle for the establishment of a fighting union between the Palestinian and Arab peoples and between all Arab liberation forces agreed on this program.

7. The Palestine national authority will strive to call on the Arab states in confrontation [with Israel] to complete the liberation of the whole of the soil of Palestine as a step on the way to comprehensive Arab unity.

8. The PLO will strive to strengthen its solidarity with the socialist countries and world forces of liberation and progress to thwart all Zionist, reactionary, and imperialist designs.

9. In the light of this program, the PLO will strive to strengthen patriotic unity and raise it to the level at which it will be able to fulfill its patriotic and national tasks and duties.

10. In the light of this program, the revolutionary command will prepare tactics which will serve and make possible the realization of these objectives.

Camp David Frameworks for Peace*

*Signed on September 17, 1985 by President Anwar Sadat of Egypt and Prime Minister Menachem Begin of Israel, and witnessed by President Jimmy Carter of the United States, at Camp David, in Thurmont, Maryland. The sections excerpted here relate to the West Bank and Gaza.

Preamble

The search for peace in the Middle East must be guided by the following:
– The agreed basis for a peaceful settlement of the conflict between Israel and its neighbors is United Nations Security Coucil Resolution 242, in all its parts.

– After four wars during thirty years, despite intensive human efforts, the Middle East, which is the cradle of civilization and the birthplace of three great religions, does not yet enjoy the blessings of peace. The people of the Middle East yearn for peace so that the vast human and natural resources of the region can be turned to the pursuits of peace and so that this area can become a model for coexistence and cooperation among nations.

– The historic initiative of President Sadat in visiting Jerusalem and the reception accorded to him by the Parliament, government and people of Israel, and the reciprocal visit of Prime Minister Begin to Ismailia, the peace proposals made by both leaders, as well as the warm reception of these missions by the people of both countries, have created an unprecedented opportunity for peace which must not be lost if this generation and future generations are to be spared the tragedies of war.

– The provisions of the Charter of the United Nations and the other accepted norms of international law and legitimacy now provide accepted standards for the conduct of relations among the states.

– To achieve a relationship of peace, in the spirit of Article 2 of the United Nations Charter, future negotiations between Israel and any neighbor prepared to negotiate peace and security with it, are necessary for the purpose of carrying out all the provisions and principles of Resolutions 242 and 338.

–Peace requires respect for the sovereignty, territorial integrity and political independence of every state in the area and their right to live in peace within secure and recognized boundaries free from threats or acts of force. Progress toward that goal can accelerate movement toward a new era of reconciliation in the Middle East marked by cooperation in promoting economic development, in maintaining stability, and in assuring security.

– Security is enhanced by a relationship of peace and by cooperation between nations which enjoy normal relations. In addition, under the terms of peace treaties, the parties can, on the basis of reciprocity, agree to special security arrangements such as demilitarized zones, limited armaments areas, early warning stations, the presence of international forces, liaison, agreed measures for monitoring, and other arrangements that they agree are useful.

Framework

Taking these factors into account, the parties are determined to reach a just, comprehensive, and durable settlement of the Middle East conflict through the conclusion of peace treaties based on Security Council Resolutions 242 and

338 in all their parts. Their purpose is to achieve peace and good neighborly relations. They recognize that, for peace to endure, it must involve all those who have been most deeply affected by the conflict. They therefore agree that this framework as appropriate is intended by them to constitute a basis for peace not only between Egypt and Israel, but also between Israel and each of its other neighbors which is prepared to negotiate peace with Israel on this basis. With that objective in mind, they have agreed to proceed as follows:

A. West Bank and Gaza

1. Egypt, Israel, Jordan and the representatives of the Palestinian people should participate in negotiations on the resolution of the Palestinian problem in all its aspects. To achieve that objective, negotiations relating to the West Bank and Gaza should proceed in three stages:

(a) Egypt and Israel agree that, in order to ensure a peaceful and orderly transfer of authority, and taking into account the security concerns of all the parties, there should be transitional arrangements for the West Bank and Gaza for a period not exceeding five years. In order to provide full autonomy to the inhabitants, under these arrangements the Israeli military government and its civilian administration will be withdrawn as soon as a self-governing authority has been freely elected by the inhabitants of these areas to replace the existing military government. To negotiate the details of a transitional arrangement, the Government of Jordan will be invited to join the negotiations on the basis of this framework. These new arrangements should give due consideration both to the principle of self-government by the inhabitants of these territories and to the legitimate security concerns of the parties involved.

(b) Egypt, Israel and Jordan will agree on the modalities for establishing the elected self-governing authority in the West Bank and Gaza. The delegations of Egypt and Jordan may include Palestinians from the West Bank and Gaza or other Palestinians as mutually agreed. The parties will negotiate an agreement which will define the powers and responsibilities of the self-governing authority to be exercised in the West Bank and Gaza. A withdrawal of Israeli armed forces will take place and there will be a redeployment of the remaining Israeli forces into specified security locations. The agreement will also include arrangements for assuring internal and external security and public order. A strong local police force will be established, which may include Jordanian citizens. In addition, Israeli and Jordanian forces will participate in joint patrols and in the manning of control posts to assure the security of the borders.

(c) When the self-governing authority (administrative council) in the West Bank and Gaza is established and inaugurated, the transitional period of five years will begin. As soon as possible, but not later than the third year after the beginning of the transitional period, negotiations will take place to determine the final status of the West Bank and Gaza and its relationship with its neighbors, and to conclude a peace treaty between Israel and Jordan by the end of the transitional period. These negotiations will be conducted among Egypt, Israel, Jordan and the elected representatives of the inhabitants of the West Bank and Gaza. Two separate but related committees will be convened, one committee, consisting of representatives of the four parties which will negotiate and agree on the final status of the West Bank and Gaza, and its relationship with its neighbors, and the second committee, consisting of representatives of Israel and representatives of Jordan to be joined by the elected representatives of the inhabitants of the West Bank and Gaza, to negotiate the peace treaty between Israel and Jordan, taking into account the agreement reached on the final status of the West Bank and Gaza. The negotiations shall be based on all the provisions and principles of UN Security Council Resolution 242. The negotiations will resolve, among other matters, the location of the boundaries and the nature of the security arrangements. The solution from the negotiations must also recognize the legitimate rights of the Palestinian people and their just requirements. In this way, the Palestinians will participate in the determination of their own future through:

1) The negotiations among Egypt, Israel, Jordan and the representatives of the inhabitants of the West Bank and Gaza to agree on the final status of the West Bank and Gaza and other outstanding issues by the end of the transitional period.

2) Submitting their agreement to a vote by the elected representatives of the inhabitants of the West Bank and Gaza.

3) Providing for the elected representatives of the inhabitants of the West Bank and Gaza to decide how they shall govern themselves consistent with the provisions of their agreement.

4) Participating as stated above in the work of the committee negotiating the peace treaty between Israel and Jordan.

All necessary measures will be taken and provisions made to assure the security of Israel and its neighbors during the transitional period and beyond. To assist in providing such security, a strong local police force will be constituted by the self-governing authority. It will be composed of inhabitants of the West Bank and Gaza. The police will maintain continuing liaison on internal security matters with the designated Israeli, Jordanian, and Egyptian officers.

During the transitional period, representatives of Egypt, Israel, Jordan, and the self-governing authority will constitute a continuing committee to decide by agreement on the modalities of admission of persons displaced from the West Bank and Gaza in 1967, together with necessary measures to prevent disruption and disorder. Other matters of common concern may also be dealt with by this committee.

Egypt and Israel will work with each other and with other interested parties to establish agreed procedures for a prompt, just and permanent implementation of the resolution of the refugee problem.

The Reagan Plan*

... The quesiton now is how to reconcile Israel's legitimate security concerns with the legitimate rights of the Palestinians. And that answer can only come at the negotiating table. Each party must recognize that the outcome must be acceptable to all and that true peace will require compromises by all.

So, tonight I am calling for a fresh start. This is the moment for all those directly concerned to get involved – or lend their support – to a workable basis for peace. The Camp David agreement remains the foundation of our policy. Its language provides all parties with the leeway they need for successful negotiations.

● I call on Israel to make clear that the security for which she yearns can only be achieved through genuine peace, a peace requiring magnanimity, vision, and courage.

● I call on the Palestinian people to recognize that their own political aspirations are inextricably bound to recognition of Israel's right to a secure future.

● And I call on the Arab states to accept the reality of Israel and the reality that peace and justice are to be gained only through hard, fair, direct negotiation.

In making these calls upon others, I recognize that the United States has a special responsibility. No other nation is in a position to deal with the key parties to the conflict on the basis of trust and reliability.

The time has come for a new realism on the part of all the peoples of the Middle East. The State of Israel is an accomplished fact; it deserves unchallenged legitimacy within the community of nations. But Israel's legitimacy has thus far been recognized by too few countries and has been denied by every Arab state except Egypt. Israel exists; it has a right to exist in peace behind secure and defensible borders; and it has a right to demand of its neighbors that they recognize those facts.

I have personally followed and supported Israel's heroic struggle for survival ever since the founding of the State of Israel 34 years ago. In the pre-1967 borders, Israel was barely 10 miles wide at its narrowest point. The bulk of Israel's population lived within artillery range of hostile Arab armies. I am not about to ask Israel to live that way again.

The war in Lebanon has demonstrated another reality in the region. The departure of the Palestinians from Beirut dramatizes more than ever the homelessness of the Palestinian people. Palestinians feel strongly that their cause is more than a question of refugees. I agree. The Camp David agreement recognized that fact when it spoke of the legitimate rights of the Palestinian

*Excerpt from a speech delivered by President Ronald Reagan on September 1, 1982, in Burbank, California.

people and their just requirements. For peace to endure, it must involve all those who have been most deeply affected by the conflict. Only through broader participation in the peace process – most immediately by Jordan and by the Palestinians – will Israel be able to rest confident in the knowledge that its security and integrity will be respected by its neighbors. Only through the process of negotiation can all the nations of the Middle East achieve a secure peace.

These then are our general goals. What are the specific new American positions, and why are we taking them?

In the Camp David talks thus far, both Israel and Egypt have felt free to express openly their views as to what the outcome should be. Understandably, their views have differed on many points.

The United States has thus far sought to play the role of mediator; we have avoided public comment on the key issues. We have always recognized – and continue to recognize – that only the voluntary agreement of those parties most directly involved in the conflict can provide an enduring solution. But it has become evident to me that some clearer sense of America's position on the key issues is necessary to encourage wider support for the peace process.

First, as outlined in the Camp David accords, there must be a period of time during which the Palestinian inhabitants of the West Bank and Gaza will have full autonomy over their own affairs. Due consideration must be given to the principle of self-government by the inhabitants of the territories and to the legitimate security concerns of the parties involved.

The purpose of the 5-year period of transition, which would begin after free elections for a self-governing Palestinian authority, is to prove to the Palestinians that they can run their own affairs and that such Palestinian autonomy poses no threat to Israel's security.

The United States will not support the use of any additional land for the purpose of settlements during the transition period. Indeed, the immediate adoption of a settlement freeze by Israel, more than any other action, could create the confidence needed for wider participation in these talks. Further settlement activity is in no way necessary for the security of Israel and only diminishes the confidence of the Arabs that a final outcome can be freely and fairly negotiated.

I want to make the American position well understood: The purpose of this transition period is the peaceful and orderly transfer of authority from Israel to the Palestinian inhabitants of the West Bank and Gaza. At the same time, such a transfer must not interfere with Israel's security requirements.

Beyond the transition period, as we look to the future of the West Bank and Gaza, it is clear to me that peace cannot be achieved by the formation of an independent Palestinian state in those territories. Nor is it achievable on the basis of Israeli sovereignty or permanent control over the West Bank and Gaza.

So the United States will not support the establishment of an independent Palestinian state in the West Bank and Gaza, and we will not support annexation or permanent control by Israel.

There is, however, another way to peace. The final status of these lands must, of course, be reached through the give-and-take of negotiations. But it is the firm view of the United States that self-government by the Palestinians of the West Bank and Gaza in association with Jordan offers the best chance for a durable, just and lasting peace.

We base our approach squarely on the principle that the Arab-Israeli conflict should be resolved through negotiations involving an exchange of territory for peace. This exchange is enshrined in U.N. Security Council Resolution 242, which is, in turn, incorporated in all its parts in the Camp David agreements. U.N. Resolution 242 remains wholly valid as the foundation stone of America's Middle East peace effort.

It is the United States' position that – in return for peace – the withdrawal provision of Resolution 242 applies to all fronts, including the West Bank and Gaza.

When the border is negotiated between Jordan and Israel, our view on the extent to which Israel should be asked to give up territory will be heavily affected by the extent of true peace and normalization and the security arrangements offered in return.

Finally, we remain convinced that Jerusalem must remain undivided, but its final status should be decided through negotiations.

In the course of the negotiations to come, the United States will support positions that seem to us fair and reasonable compromises and likely to promote a sound agreement. We will also put forward our own detailed proposals when we believe they can be helpful. And, make no mistake, the United States will oppose any proposal – from any party and at any point in the negotiating process – that threatens the security of Israel. America's commitment to the security of Israel is ironclad. And, I might add, so is mine.

THE PALESTINE MANDATE, 1920

ARMISTICE LINES, 1949

Map labels:

MEDITERRANEAN SEA

Afula

Jenin

Hadera

SAMARIA

Netanya

Tulkarm

Elon Moreh

Kedumim

Qalqiliya

Nablus

Herzliyya

Emanuel

Tappuah

Elkana

Ma'aleh Efraim

TEL AVIV JAFFA

Ariel

Petah Tikva

Shiloh

Ofra

Rishon Le-Ziyyon

Lod

Beth El

Ramallah

Ramla

Givat Ze'ev

Jericho

Rehovot

KINGDOM OF JORDAN

Ashdod

JERUSALEM

Ma'aleh Adumim

Har Gilo

Bethlehem

Kaliya

ISRAEL

Alon Shvut

Tekoah

DEAD SEA

Kfar Etzion

Hebron

Kiryat Arba

JUDEA

Yatir

Jordan River

Dhahiriya

Beersheba

B. Petersen
INTERARTS

NORTH

☆ = Jewish Settlements in the West Bank
● = Main Arab towns in the West Bank
▨ = Annexed by Israel, 1967
-∙- = 1949 Armistice Line
━━ = Main roads

0   10   20
miles

THE WEST BANK

161

Background Sources and Readings

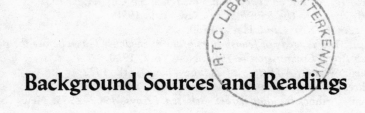

In the facts and analyses it offers, as well as in the conversations it reports, this book touches upon a wide span of history and experience, both Jewish and Arab, that it makes no attempt to adequately develop or summarize. Numerous sources exist, however, both primary and secondary, that do so, many of them with conflicting viewpoints and approaches. The following list includes some of those sources, categorized according to several of the themes emerging from this book. Information about contemporary views and events in Israel can be followed in English on a weekly basis in the *Jerusalem Post International Edition* (North American subscriptions available from P.O. Box 2000, Patterson, New York 12563; other subscriptions from P.O. Box 81, Jerusalem 91000, Israel). Corresponding information about views and events in the West Bank and Gaza, as well as in the Palestinian community outside of those areas, can be followed, also in English, in the *Al-Fajr Jerusalem Palestinian Weekly* (North American subscriptions available from 16 Crowell Street, Hempstead, New York 11550; other subscriptions from *Al-Fajr*, Hatem al-Ta'ee Street, Jerusalem). Longer articles about the Palestinian Arab cause may be found in the *Journal of Palestine Studies*.

1. Zionism and the Founders of Modern Israel

Ahad HaAm. *Selected Essays.* Philadelphia, 1948.
_____ . *Ten Essays on Zionism and Judaism.* London, 1922.
Berlin, Isaiah. *The Life and Opinions of Moses Hess.* Cambridge, Mass., 1959.
Elon, Amos. *Herzl.* New York, 1975.
Gordon, A.D. *Selected Essays.* New York, 1938.

Halkin, Abraham S., ed. *Zionism in Jewish Literature.* New York, 1961.

Hertzberg, Arthur, ed. *The Zionist Idea.* Garden City, N.Y., 1959.

Herzl, Theodor. *The Jewish State.* New York, 1970.

———. *Old-New Land.* Haifa, 1960.

———. *The Tragedy of Jewish Immigration: Evidence Given before the British Royal Commission in 1902.* New York, 1920.

Laqueur, Walter. *A History of Zionism.* New York, 1972.

Pinsker, Leo. *Auto-Emancipation.* New York, 1956.

Ruppin, Arthur. *Building Israel: Selected Essays, 1907–1935.* New York, 1949.

Sachar, Howard M. *A History of Israel.* New York, 1979.

———. *Aliyah: The Peoples of Israel.* Cleveland, 1961.

Samuel, Maurice. *Harvest in the Desert.* New York, 1944.

Sanders, Ronald. *Israel: The View from Masada.* New York, 1966.

Schechtman, Joseph B. *Vladimir Jabotinsky,* 2 vols. New York, 1956–61.

Shazar, Zalman. *Morning Stars.* Philadelphia, 1967.

Tchernichowsky, Saul. *Selected Poems.* London, 1929.

Weizmann, Chaim. *Trial and Error.* New York, 1949.

2. Palestine from Biblical Times to the British Mandate

Aharoni, Yohonan, and Michael Avi-Yonah. *The Macmillan Bible Atlas,* revised ed. New York, 1968.

Ben-Zvi, Yitzhak. *Israel under Ottoman Rule—Four Centuries of History.* Jerusalem, 1955.

Farhi, David. "Ottoman Attitude Towards Jewish Settlement." In Moshe Ma'oz, ed., *Studies on Palestine during the Ottoman Period.* Jerusalem, 1975.

Grollenberg, Luc. H. *The Penguin Shorter Atlas of the Bible.* London, 1978.

Josephus, Flavius. *The Complete Works of Flavius Josephus, the Celebrated Jewish Historian.* Trans. W. Whiston. Philadelphia, 1895.

Parkes, James. *A History of Palestine from 135 A.D. to Modern Times.* London, 1949.

———. *Whose Land? History of the Peoples of Palestine.* London, 1970.

Peters, Joan. *From Time Immemorial: The Origins of the Arab-Jewish Conflict over Palestine.* New York, 1984.

Rhymer, Joseph. *Atlas of the Biblical World.* New York, 1982.

Wilson, C.T. *Peasant Life in the Holyland.* London, 1906.

3. The Balfour Declaration and the British Mandate for Palestine

Abdullah, King of Jordan. *Memoirs.* New York, 1950.

———. *My Memoirs Completed.* Washington, D.C., 1954.

Anglo-American Committee of Inquiry. *A Survey of Palestine*, 3 vols. Palestine, 1945–1946.

―――. *Report to the United States Government and His Majesty's Government in the United Kingdom*. Lausanne, Switzerland, April 20, 1946. Washington, D.C., 1946.

Antonius, George. *The Arab Awakening*. Philadelphia, 1938.

Arab Higher Committee for Palestine. *A Collection of Official Documents Relating to the Palestine Question 1917–1947*. Submitted to the General Assembly of the United Nations, November 1947.

―――. *Memorandum Submitted to the Royal Commission on January 11, 1937*. Jerusalem, 1937.

Aumann, Moshe. *Land Ownership in Palestine, 1880–1948*. Jerusalem, 1976.

Balfour, Arthur James. *Speeches on Zionism*. London, 1928.

Bauer, Yehuda. *From Diplomacy to Resistance: A History of Jewish Palestine, 1939–1945*. Philadelphia, 1970.

Ben-Gurion, David. *The Peel Report and the Jewish State*. Jerusalem, 1938.

Bentwich, Norman and Helen. *Mandate Memories, 1918–1948*. London, 1965.

Bernadotte, Folke. *To Jerusalem*. London, 1951.

Boustany, W.F. *The Palestine Mandate: Invalid and Impracticable*. Beirut, 1936.

Buber, Martin, Judah L. Magnes, and Moses Smilansky. *Palestine: A Bi-National State*. New York, 1946.

Canaan, Tawfiq. *Conflict in the Land of Peace*. Jerusalem, 1936.

Churchill, Winston S. *The World Crisis*, vol. 4. London, 1929.

Gilbert, Martin. *The Arab-Israeli Conflict: Its History in Maps*. London, 1974.

―――. *Winston S. Churchill, The Prophet of Truth: 1922–1939*, 5 vols. Boston, 1977.

Glubb, Lieutenant General Sir John B. *A Soldier with the Arabs*. London, 1957.

Great Britain. *Palestine Partition Report* (Woodhead Report). Command No. 5854. London, 1938.

―――. *Palestine: Report on Immigration, Land Settlement and Development* (Hope Simpson Report). Command Nos. 3686–7. 2 vols. London, 1930.

―――. *Palestine: Royal Commission Report* (Peel Report). Command No. 5479. London, 1937.

―――. *Palestine: Statement of Policy* (White Paper). Command No. 6019. London, 1939.

Hattis, Susan Lee. *The Bi-National Idea in Palestine During Mandatory Times*. Jerusalem, 1970.

Hourani, Albert. *Great Britain and the Arab World*. London, 1945.

Hurewitz, J.C. *The Struggle for Palestine*. New York, 1950.

Hyamson, Albert. *Palestine under the Mandate*. London, 1950.

Ingrams, Doreen. *Palestine Papers, 1917–1922: Seeds of Conflict*. London, 1972.

Jabotinsky, Vladimir. *The Story of the Jewish Legion*. New York, 1945.

Jewish Agency. *The Jewish Case Against the White Paper: Documents Submitted to the Permanent Mandates Commission*. London, 1939.

———. *Palestine: Land Settlement, Urban Development and Immigration. Memorandum to Sir John Hope Simpson, July 1930*. London, 1930.

Jewish Frontier Association. *The Broken Pledge: The Case Against the White Paper of Palestine*. New York, 1944.

Joseph, Bernard. *British Rule in Palestine*. Washington, D.C., 1948.

Kedourie, Elie. *Britain and the Middle East, 1914–1921*. London, 1956.

Khalidi, Thabit al-. *Arab Clan Rivalry in Palestine*. Jerusalem, 1945.

Kimche, Jon. *The Second Arab Awakening*. London, 1970.

———. *Seven Fallen Pillars: The Middle East 1915–1950*. London, 1950.

Kirkbride, Sir Alan. *A Crackle of Thorns*. London, 1956.

Koestler, Arthur. *Promise and Fulfillment: Palestine 1917–1949*. London, 1949.

Laqueur, Walter, ed. *The Israel-Arab Reader*. New York, 1969.

Laserson, Max M., ed. *On the Mandate: Documents, Statements, Laws and Judgments Relating to and Arising from the Mandate for Palestine*. Tel Aviv, 1937.

Meinertzhagen, Richard. *Middle East Diary, 1917–1956*. London, 1959.

Porath, Yehoshua. *The Emergence of the Palestinian-Arab National Movement, 1918–1929*. London, 1974.

Rihani, Amin. *The Fate of Palestine*. Beirut, 1967.

Sachar, Howard M. *The Emergence of the Middle East*. New York, 1969.

Samuel, Viscount Herbert L.S. *Memoirs*. London, 1955.

Samuel, Maurice. *On the Rim of the Wilderness: The Conflict in Palestine*. New York, 1931.

Sanders, Ronald. *The High Walls of Jerusalem: A History of the Balfour Declaration and the Birth of the British Mandate for Palestine*. New York, 1984.

Sayegh, Fayez. *Zionist Colonization of Palestine*. Beirut, 1965.

Sykes, Christopher. *Crossroads to Israel, 1917–1948*. New York, 1965.

Tibawi, Abdul Latif. *Arab Education in Mandatory Palestine*. London, 1956.

Waters, M.P. *Mufti over the Middle East*. London, 1942.

4. The Creation of the State of Israel

Begin, Menachem. *The Revolt: Story of the Irgun*. New York, 1951.

Ben-Gurion, David. *Israel: A Personal History*. New York, 1971.

Ben-Gurion, David. *Rebirth and Destiny of Israel*. New York, 1954.

Bethell, Nicholas. *The Palestine Triangle: The Struggle for the Holy Land, 1935–48.* New York, 1979.

Bishuit, Bassam. *The Role of the Zionist Terror in the Creation of Israel.* Beirut, 1969.

Elon, Amos. *The Israelis: Fathers and Sons.* New York, 1971.

Gilbert, Martin. *The Jews of Arab Lands: Their History in Maps.* Oxford, 1975.

Goldmann, Nahum. *Sixty Years of Jewish Life.* New York, 1969.

Great Britain. *Proposals for the Future of Palestine: July, 1946–February, 1947.* Command No. 7044. London, 1947.

————. *Report of the Anglo-American Committee of Inquiry Regarding the Problems of European Jewry and Palestine, Lausanne, 20th April, 1946.* Command No. 6808. London, 1946.

Hilberg, Raoul. *The Destruction of the European Jews.* Chicago, 1961.

Hurewitz, J.C. *The Struggle for Palestine.* New York, 1950.

Kimche, Jon. *There Could Have Been Peace.* New York, 1973.

Kimche, Jon and David. *The Secret Road: The "Illegal" Migration of a People, 1938–48.* London, 1954.

————. *Both Sides of the Hill: Britain and the Palestine War.* London, 1960.

Kurzman, Dan. *The First Arab-Israeli War.* Cleveland, 1970.

Lucas, Noah. *The Modern History of Israel.* London, 1975.

Meir, Golda. *My Life.* New York, 1975.

Pearlman, Maurice. *Mufti of Jerusalem: The Story of Haj Amin al-Husseini.* London, 1947.

Sachar, Howard M. *Europe Leaves the Middle East.* New York, 1972.

Schechtman, Joseph B. *The Mufti and the Führer.* New York, 1965.

Stone, I.F. *Underground to Palestine.* New York, 1946; reissued with a new Introduction and Epilogue, New York, 1978.

————. *This Is Israel.* New York, 1948.

5. Israel as Polity, Society, and Culture

Abramov, S.Z. *Perpetual Dilemma: Jewish Religion in the Jewish State.* Cranbury, N.J., 1976.

Agnon, S.Y. *A Guest for the Night.* London, 1968.

Antonovsky, Aaron, and Alan Arian. *Hopes and Fears of Israelis.* Jerusalem, 1972.

Asmar, Fouzi el-. *To Be an Arab in Israel.* London, 1975.

Bachi, Roberto. *The Population of Israel.* Jerusalem, 1974.

Badi, Joseph. *The Government of the State of Israel.* New York, 1963.

————. *Religion in Israel Today: The Relationship Between State and Religion.* New York, 1969.

Ben-Porath, Yoram. *The Arab Labor Force in Israel.* Jerusalem, 1966.

Eisenstadt, S.N. *Israeli Society.* London, 1967.

Jiryis, Sabri. *Democratic Freedoms in Israel*. Beirut, 1972.

————. *The Arabs in Israel*. Beirut, 1969.

Kanovsky, E. *The Economic Impact of the Six-Day War*. New York, 1970.

Landau, Jacob. *The Arabs in Israel*. London, 1969.

Oz, Amos. *Elsewhere, Perhaps*. New York, 1972.

————. *My Michael*. New York, 1972.

Perlmutter, Amos. *Military and Politics in Israel*. London, 1969.

Rosetti, Moshe. *The Knesset: Its Origins, Forms, and Procedures*. Jerusalem, 1966.

Selzer, Michael. *The Outcasts of Israel: Communal Tensions in the Jewish State*. Jerusalem, 1965.

Smooha, Sami. *Israel, Pluralism and Conflict*. London, 1978.

6. Israel Among the Arab States

Alroy, Gil Carl. *Behind the Middle East Conflict: The Real Impasse Between Arab and Jew*. New York, 1975.

Avineri, Shlomo, ed. *Israel and the Palestinians*. New York, 1971.

Bell, W. Bowyer. *The Long War: Israel and the Arabs since 1946*. Englewood Cliffs, N.J., 1969.

Blum, Yehuda Z. *Secure Boundaries and Middle East Peace*. Jerusalem, 1971.

Cohen, Aharon. *Israel and the Arab World*. New York, 1970.

Dodd, Ch.H., and Mary Sales, eds. *Israel and the Arab World*. London, 1970.

Hadawi, Sami. *Crime and No Punishment: Zionist Israeli Terrorism, 1939–1972*. Beirut, 1972.

Harkabi, Yehoshafat. *Arab Attitudes to Israel*. Jerusalem, 1972.

————. *Palestinians and Israel*. Jerusalem, 1974.

————. *The Palestinian Covenant and Its Meaning*. London, 1979.

Heykal, Mohammed Hassanein. *The Cairo Documents*. New York, 1973.

————. *The Road to Ramadan*. New York, 1975.

Horowitz, Dan, and M. Lissak. *The Origin of the Israeli Polity*. Chicago, 1979.

Hourani, Albert, and J.L. Talmon. *Israel and the Arabs*. London, 1967.

Hussein, King of Jordan. *Uneasy Lies the Head*. New York, 1962.

Kerr, Malcolm H. *Regional Arab Politics and the Conflict with Israel*. Santa Monica, Calif., 1969.

Khouri, Fred J. *The Arab-Israeli Dilemma*. Syracuse, N.Y., 1968.

Moore, John Morton. *The Arab-Israeli Conflict; Readings and Documents*. Princeton, N.J., 1977.

Rabinovitch, Itamar and Jehuda Reinharz (eds.). *Israel in the Middle East*. New York, 1984.

Robinson, Donald B. *Under Fire: Israel's Twenty-Year Struggle for Survival*. New York, 1968.

Safran, Nadav. *From War to War: The Arab-Israeli Confrontation, 1948–1967*. New York, 1969.

Schiff, Ze'ev, and Raphael Rothstein. *Fedayeen*. London, 1972.

Talmon, J.L. *Israel among the Nations*. London, 1970.

7. The Six-Day War

Abu-Lughod, Ibrahim. *The Arab-Israeli Confrontation of June 1967: An Arab Perspective*. Evanston, Ill., 1970.

Associated Press. *Lightning out of Israel: The Six-Day War in the Middle East*. New York, 1967.

Bar-On, Mordecai. *Israel Defense Forces: The Six-Day War*. Philadelphia, 1969.

Draper, Theodore. *Israel and World Politics: Roots of the Third Arab-Israeli War*. London, 1968.

Khalidi, Ahmad Samih el-. *The Arab-Israeli War, 1967*. Beirut, 1969.

Lall, Arthur. *The United Nations and the Middle East Crisis, 1967*. New York, 1968.

Nutting, Anthony. *Nasser*. New York, 1972.

Rabinovich, Abraham. *The Battle for Jerusalem, June 5–7, 1967*. Philadelphia, 1972.

Samo, Elias. *The June 1967 Arab-Israeli War*. Illinois, 1971.

Schleifer, Abdullah. *The Fall of Jerusalem*. New York, 1972.

Vance, Vic, and Pierre Lauer. *Hussein of Jordan: My "War" with Israel*. New York, 1969.

8. The Palestinian Arab Experience and the Response to Zionism

Abboushi, W.F. *The Angry Arabs*. Philadelphia, 1974.

Abid, Ibrahim al-. *Israel and Human Rights*. Beirut, 1969.

———. *A Handbook to the Palestine Question*. Beirut, 1969.

———. *Selected Essays on the Palestine Question*. Beirut, 1969.

Abu-Lughod, Ibrahim. *The Transformation of Palestine*. Evanston, Ill., 1971.

———. *Altered Realities: The Palestinians since 1967*. North Dartmouth, Mass., 1972.

Chiha, Michel. *Palestine*. Beirut, 1969.

Darwaza, Al-Hakam. *The Palestine Question: A Brief Analysis*. Beirut, 1973.

Dimbleby, Jonathan. *The Palestinians*. London, 1979.

Dodd, Peter, and Halim Barakat. *River Without Bridges: A Study of the Exodus of the 1967 Palestinian Arab Refugees*. Beirut, 1969.

Epp, Frank H. *The Palestinians*. Scottsdale, Penn., 1976.

Frangi, Abdallah. *The PLO and Palestine*. London, 1983.

Furlonge, Sir Geoffrey. *Palestine Is My Country: The Story of Musa Alami*. New York, 1969.

Gilmour, David. *The Dispossessed: The Ordeal of the Palestinians, 1917–1980*. London, 1980.

Hadawi, Sami. *Bitter Harvest: Palestine Between 1914–1946*. New York, 1967.

_____ . *Palestine: Loss of a Heritage*. San Antonio, 1963.

Institute for Palestine Studies. *The Palestinian Refugees: A Collection of United Nations Documents*. Beirut, 1970.

Iyad, Abu, with Eric Rouleau. *My Home, My Land: A Narrative of the Palestinian Struggle*. New York, 1978.

John, Robert, and Sami Hadawi. *The Palestine Diary*. New York, 1970.

Kadi, Leila S. *Arab Summit Conferences and the Palestine Problem*. Beirut, 1966.

_____ . *Basic Political Documents of the Armed Palestinian Resistance Movement*. Beirut, 1969.

Kayyali, Abdul-Wahhab Said. *Palestine: A Modern History*. London, 1978.

Khaled, Leila. *My People Shall Live*. London, 1973.

Kishtainy, Khalid. *Whither Israel? A Study of Zionist Expansionism*. Beirut. 1970.

Ma'oz, Moshe. *The Image of the Jew in Official Arab Literature and Communications Media*. Jerusalem, 1976.

Nazzal, Nafez. *The Palestinian Exodus from Galilee, 1948*. Beirut, 1978.

Palestine Research Center. *Palestine Leaders Discuss the New Challenges for the Resistance*. Beirut, 1974.

Pinner, Walter. *How Many Arab Refugees?* New York, 1953.

_____ . *The Legend of the Arab Refugees*. Tel Aviv, 1967.

Porath, Y. *The Emergence of the Palestinian Arab National Movement 1918–1929*. London, 1974.

Quandt, William B., Fuad Jabber, and Ann Mosley Lesch. *The Politics of Palestinian Nationalism*. Berkeley, 1973.

_____ . *Palestinian Nationalism: Its Political and Military Dimensions*. Santa Monica, Calif., 1971.

Rasheed, Muhammad. *Toward a Democratic State in Palestine*. Beirut, 1970.

Razzaq, Asad. *Greater Israel: A Study in Zionist Expansionist Thought*. Beirut, 1970.

Said, Edward. *The Question of Palestine*. New York, 1980.

Sakhnini, Isam. *P.L.O.: The Representative of the Palestinians*. Beirut, 1974.

Sayigh, Rosemary. *Palestinians: From Peasants to Revolutionaries*. London, 1979.

Sharabi, Hisham. *Palestine and Israel: The Lethal Dilemma*. New York, 1969.

_____ . *Palestine Guerrillas: Their Credibility and Effectiveness*. Washington, D.C., 1970.

Turki, Fawaz. *The Disinherited: Journal of a Palestinian Exile*. New York and London, 1972.

Zurayk, Constantine. *The Meaning of the Disaster*. Beirut, 1960.

9. Israel in the West Bank and Gaza

Amnesty International. *Report on the Treatment of Certain Prisoners under Interrogation in Israel.* London, 1970.

Ben-Porath, Yoram, and Emanuel Marx. *Some Sociological and Economic Aspects of Refugee Camps in the West Bank.* Santa Monica, Calif., 1971.

Benvenisti, Meron. *The West Bank and Gaza Data Base Project; Interim Report No. 1.* Jerusalem, 1982.

――――. *The West Bank Data Project: A Survey of Israel's Policies.* Washington, D.C., 1984.

Blum, Yehuda Z. "The Missing Reversioner: Reflections on the Status of Judea and Samaria," *Israel Law Review,* vol. 3 (1968), pp. 293–294.

Bregman, Arye. *The Economy of the Administered Territories, 1974 and 1975.* Jerusalem, 1976.

Davis, U., A. E. L. Marks, and J. Richardson. "Israel Water Policies," *Journal of Palestine Studies,* vol. 9, no. 2 (Winter 1980), pp. 3–31.

Drobles, Mattityahu. *Settlement in Judea and Samaria.* Jerusalem, 1980.

Elazar, Daniel J. *Self-Rule/Shared Rule.* Ramat Gan, Israel, 1979.

――――. *Judea, Samaria, and Gaza: Views on the Present and Future.* Washington, D.C., 1982.

Gavron, Daniel. *Israel After Begin: Israel's Options in the Aftermath of the Lebanese War.* Boston, 1984.

Harkabi, Y. *Arab Strategies and Israel's Responses.* Detroit, 1976.

Heller, Mark A. *A Palestinian State.* Cambridge, Mass., 1983.

Hochstein, Annette. *Metropolitan Links between Israel and the West Bank.* Jerusalem, 1980.

Institute for Palestine Studies. *Israel and the Geneva Conventions.* Beirut, 1968.

Israel, the Brutal Occupier. The Red Cross Testifies. Beirut, 1972.

Israel National Section of the International Commission of Jurists. *The Rule of Law in the Areas Administered by Israel.* Tel Aviv, 1981.

Kenan, Amos. *Israel: A Wasted Victory.* Tel Aviv, 1970.

Kuttab, Jonathan, and Rajah Shehadeh. *Civilian Administration in the Occupied West Bank.* Ramallah, 1982.

Langer, Felicia. *With My Own Eyes.* London, 1975.

Lerner, Abba, and Haim Ben Shahar. *The Economics of Efficiency and Growth: Lessons from Israel and the West Bank.* Cambridge, Mass., 1975.

Lesch, Ann Mosely. *Israel's Occupation of the West Bank: The First Two Years.* Santa Monica, Calif., 1970.

Oz, Amos. *In the Land of Israel.* New York, 1983.

Rodinson, Maxime. *Israel: A Colonialist Settler State?* New York, 1974.

Rosen, Steven J. *Military Geography and the Military Balance in the Arab-Israel Conflict.* Jerusalem, 1976.

Singer, Joel. "The Establishment of a Civil Administration in the Areas Administered by Israel." In *Israel Yearbook on Human Rights,* Tel Aviv, 1982.

State of Israel, Ministry of Defence, Coordinator of Government Operations in Judea-Samaria and the Gaza District. *Judea-Samaria and the Gaza District—A Sixteen-Year Survey (1967–1983).* Jerusalem, 1983.

State of Israel, Ministry of Labour and Social Affairs, Department of International Relations. *Labour and Employment in Judea and Samaria, Gaza and Sinai: A Survey of the Activities of the Ministry of Labour and Social Affairs during 1967–1979.* Jerusalem, 1980.

United States Senate, Committee on the Judiciary. *The Colonization of the West Bank Territories by Israel.* Washington, D.C.: Hearings Before the Subcommittee on Immigration and Naturalization, October 17–18, 1977.

Van Arkadie, Brian. *Benefits and Burdens: A Report on the West Bank and Gaza Strip Economies since 1967.* Washington, D.C., 1977.

10. The Palestinians in the West Bank and Gaza

Abid, Ibrahim al-. *Human Rights in the Occupied Territories.* Beirut, 1970.
_____. *Israel and Human Rights.* Beirut, 1969.
Arab Areas Occupied by Israel in June 1967. North Dartmouth, Mass., 1970.
The Arabs under Israeli Occupation, 1976–1979. Beirut, 1979.
Artawi, Hisham. *A Survey of Industries in the West Bank and the Gaza Strip.* Bir Zeit, 1979.
_____. *West Bank Agriculture: A New Outlook.* Nablus, 1978.
Bull, Vivian A. *The West Bank: Is It Viable?* Lexington, Mass., 1975.
Collard, Elizabeth, and R. Wilson. *The Economic Potential of an Independent Palestine.* London, 1975.
Fawdah, Izz al-Din. *Israel's Belligerent Occupation and Palestinian Armed Resistance in International Law.* Beirut, 1970.
Hilal, Jamil. *The West Bank: Its Social and Economic Structure, 1948–1973.* Beirut, 1975.
Israel's Occupation of Palestine and Other Territories. North Dartmouth, Mass., 1970.
Mishal, Shaul. *West Bank/East Bank: The Palestinians in Jordan, 1949–1967.* New Haven, 1978.
Tawil, Ramonda Hawa. *My Home My Prison.* New York, 1979.

11. Contemporary Religious Zionism and the Land of Israel

Bleich, J. David. "Judea and Samaria: Settlement and Return," *Tradition,* vol. 18, no. 1 (1979), pp. 44–78.

Eldad, Israel. *The Jewish Revolution*. New York, 1971.

Fisch, Harold. *The Zionist Revolution: A New Perspective*. New York, 1978.

Kaplan, Lawrence. "Divine Promises: Conditional and Absolute," *Tradition*, vol. 18, no. 1 (1979), pp. 35–43.

Kook, Abraham Isaac. *Abraham Isaac Kook: The Light of Penitence, The Moral Principles, Light of Holiness, Essays, Letters and Poems*. New York, 1978.

Lamm, Norman. "The Ideology of the Neturei Karta: According to the Satmerer Version," *Tradition*, vol. 13, no. 1 (1971), pp. 38–53.

Lichtenstein, Aharon. "The Ideology of Hesder," *Tradition*, vol. 19, no. 3 (1981), pp. 199–217.

Roth, Sol. "The Right to the Land," *Tradition*, vol. 16, no. 5 (1977), pp. 7–22.

Rubinstein, Amnon. *The Zionist Dream Revisited: From Herzl to Gush Emunim and Back*. New York, 1984.

Schnall, David J. "Religion, Ideology and Dissent in Contemporary Israeli Politics," *Tradition*, vol. 18, no. 1 (1979), pp. 13–34.

Walfish, Benjamin. "Gush Emunim—Faith and Hope," *Tradition*, vol. 19, no. 4 (1981), pp. 311–321.

Weiss, David W. "Planting Cherries at Keshet," *Tradition*, vol. 17, no. 3 (1978), pp. 35–50.

World Zionist Organization. *Whose Homeland? Eretz Israel: Roots of the Claim*. Number 4 of the series Contemporary Thinking in Israel, Avner Tomaschoff, general editor. Jerusalem, 1978.

Index